Walking from Garstang and in Wyresdale

by Ian and Krysia Brodie

D0264515

Carnegie Publishing, 1994

NB. Whilst every care is taken in the preparation of this book to ensure accuracy,
walkers are advised to make use of the appropriate Ordnance Survey maps to locate
precise routes. Please keep to the authorised footpaths described in the text and respect
the privacy of the residents whose properties you pass on your way.
For the benefit of future walkers please notify any footpath obstructions to the County
Surveyor and Bridgemaster, County Hall, Preston.

Walking from Garstang and in Wyresdale
Ian O. Brodie

Published by Carnegie Publishing Ltd., 18 Maynard St, Preston

Typeset in Monotype Ehrhardt by Carnegie Publishing
Printed in the UK by T. Snape & Co. Ltd, Preston

ISBN 0-948789-98-0

Contents

Introduction

This third edition of Walking from Garstang and in Wyresdale is being published because the first two editions have sold out and the book is still, we are informed, in demand. As with all walking books, changes in the landscape mean that route descriptions are soon out of date and new editions are essential to encompass these changes. This edition not only covers these changes, but contains more walks and still provides some flexibility in the length of walks.

This edition covers the whole of Wyresdale virtually from source to sea. The flavour of the river in all the different types of terrain through which it flows is included. The original walks, within easy reach of Garstang but outside the main river catchment, are still here. Most of the walks can be started from bus routes, although in one or two cases it is by an irregular service.

The area is not only one of fine, contrasting landscapes but one where history, wildlife and industrial archaeology abound. It is a walkers' mecca where field paths give rise to ever changing vistas. Luckily, most of the field paths used are free from obstruction, and this makes the way easier, and reminds us of the goodwill that we have received from many farmers and landowners who are used to seeing the earlier editions clutched in the hands of many who have chosen to follow its walks. At the request of some readers we have included, at the end of each paragraph, a general idea of what distance the route description in each paragraph covers on the ground.

We must add that carrying the respective Ordnance Survey Pathfinder maps will bring greater enjoyment to the walks and will help to clarify the routes further—the sketch maps are only illustrative. As all local people already know, rainy periods turn many of these field paths into a soggy, clay mess which demands wellingtons rather than boots.

We feel sure that readers of this book aim to enjoy the countryside and will, hopefully, find rejoinders about the country code as preaching to the converted. If you find problems with footpath blockages please let Lancashire County Council know, and if you have problems with the text please tell us, via the publisher, and we can take them into account if we are around to undertake a fourth edition!

Ian and Krysia Brodie

Nicky Nook—a perennial favourite

Garstang—Grizedale—Nicky Nook Fell—Scorton—Garstang

12 kilometres (7.5 miles)

A shorter route is indicated in the introductory paragraph

Start: Garstang Community Centre car park (GR: 493454)

O.S. Pathfinder Map 668 (SD 44/54) Garstang

THIS IS THE CLASSIC ROUTE for walkers from Garstang, despite the need to use short sections of road. It encompasses a taste of the local fells and woodlands and, regardless of Grizedale's reservoir, provides a delectable combination of all those elements of landscape that make countryside attractive. A shorter route can be undertaken by starting and finishing at Scorton and missing out the Garstang to Woodacre crossing sections.

From the car park, edge round the playing fields by the river, climb the steps up to the bridge and cross the River Wyre. (370m)

The name Wyre is possibly a Celtic derivative of the Welsh 'Gwyar' meaning blood water, a description of the reddish brown colour of the river in spate.

The bridge crosses the extraction point for water from the Lune–Wyre Conjunctive Use Scheme and from here it is piped to the Frank Law Treatment Works at Catterall. Upstream is one of the flood barriers that close when exceptional flood comes down the river. These fields act as a basin and, it is hoped, save the villages downstream from flooding.

Over the bridge where the embankments join go down left to a stile and then cross the field to a stile. Continue in the same direction in the next field to a wooden stile in the right-hand fence near the field corner. Continue in the next field to cross to the far boundary which you then follow on your left to a stile and gate. (500m)

Go right over the stile, along the lane, keep left at the junction and almost immediately cross a bridge to find a stile on your left. Cross the middle of the field (in wet weather a slight diversion towards the left may be needed) to a footbridge in the hedge, and, when over follow the right-hand fence, cross a stile and continue along the fence until it bends away to your right. (500m)

Go right and cross to a kissing-gate by a gate to the left of the wood, go through and keep near to the left-hand fence and then make for the gate in the wall. Through the gate cross the road to the right and go down the track to the left of the industrial

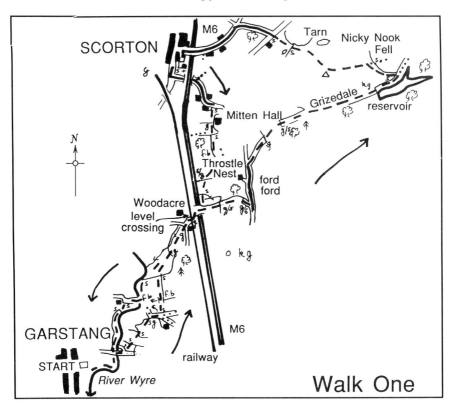

building, following a short track to the level crossing—cross with care and phone the signalman if necessary. (750m)

Continue over the motorway bridge and then keep ahead to cross the stile by a gate and reach the right-hand side of a wood. Follow the left-hand fence by the wood down to a further stile and gate and on to reach a minor road which is followed left across two streams. Pass Throstle Nest Farm on the left and, as the road begins to climb, go right down a track to a gate. Continue up the track, via a gate with a stile and, much further up, a further gate and kissing-gate along Grizedale to reach the reservoir. (2800m)

Grizedale was dammed in 1861–3. It is a peaceful scene and of some wildlife interest but in terms of lakes it is biologically unproductive: lacking nutrients and being acidic, it supports little aquatic life. The name Grizedale was given the to dale by the Norse, and it means valley of the wild pigs.

Continue along the track until a break in the left-hand fence gives access to a stile in the wall almost opposite the reservoir fork. Cross and climb the steep path keeping near the wall until a large stile crosses the wall. Do not cross but go left along the track to reach the triangulation pillar on top of Nicky Nook Fell at a height of 215 metres. (850m)

From here extensive views of Morecambe Bay, Lakeland Fells and the Forest of Bowland can be enjoyed.

Continue along the ridge and eventually bear down right to meet a wall on the nearside of the tarn. Go left as the path descends by the right-hand fence and wall, passes over a stile beside the small reservoir, and then descends more steeply to a stile to the right of the house by the road junction. Follow the quiet road that faces you all the way down to Scorton. (2000m)

Scorton is an attractive village, many of whose older properties are built of local stone. Refreshments are invariably available from the café and stores.

Scorton parish church is a typical Paley and Austin design—solid and stone-built, a reflection of Victorian values—built in 1878–9 for £14,000. It is dedicated to St Peter.

Opposite the post office and shop and Priory Café is the war memorial, and a lane which you follow down to the church. Enter the churchyard under the lychgate, go to the right of the tower to find a small gate in the wall. Through the gate go down the field, past an oak tree, to a further gate and the road (there is a public convenience just across the road to the right). (270m)

Turn left along the road, go left at the junction by the bowling green and tennis court, under the motorway, and continue along this road to a group of houses on the left-hand bend. After the last house on your right (East Barn) look for a stile in the hedge as the road climbs. This is at the end of the garden and by a road sign on your right. (550m)

In the field, aim across parallel to the motorway to pick up the left-hand hedge that fronts Mitten Hall. Continue along by the hedge to two gates in the far left-hand corner of the field. Go through the gate ahead and aim for a stile to the left of the wood corner. Over this stile follow the right-hand fence of the wood until a footbridge and stile admit you to the wood. Turn left and follow the track through the wood to a gate and stile. (900m)

Cross the stile to enter a field and make for a stile near the motorway. Cross the stile and follow the path through the gorse to a footbridge. Climb the embankment to cross the motorway bridge and railway and re-enter the fields by the gate in the wall facing you across the road, and which you previously used on the outward journey. (300m)

Go ahead across the field to the gate and kissing gate to the right of the wood. Through the gate go across the field, aiming to the right of the white bridge to climb the riverside hillock (Broom Hill) which you then descend by two stiles into the riverside field. Go along the bank to pass the Thirlmere aqueduct and cross the following footbridge. (1000m)

Continue up the lane but cross the stile on your left and then follow the path beside the right-hand fence to a stile by the river. The riverside path returns you to your start in Garstang. (1000m)

Amongst pheasants

A. Garstang—Barnacre—Garstang
7.5 kilometres (4.5 miles) or
B. Garstang—Lady Hamilton's Well (Barnacre)—Garstang
5 kilometres (3 miles)
Start: Garstang Community Centre Car Park (GR 453454)
O.S. Pathfinder map 668 (SD 44/54) Garstang

THESE WALKS are mostly on land owned by one estate. Although the owner lives abroad, the estate is well managed and combines agriculture, forestry and pheasant shooting, while still welcoming walkers on the footpaths. Pheasants will be under your feet and often rabbits as well. There are extensive views of the Lakeland fells, of Morecambe Bay and of the Fylde, so choose a clear day, preferably when the fells are starched with snow. Autumn colours in the woodlands also add interest, but beware of times when the fieldpaths are at their wettest—wellies are at a premium.

Both walks follow the same route to Barnacre Church. Leave the car park and follow the river upstream by the path and then ascend the steps in the embankment to gain access to the bridge. (500m)

The bridge occupies the site of that followed by the old Garstang to Knott End railway—the 'Pilling Pig'. It never paid its way. It usually used second-hand locomotives, and many of its buildings were no more than simple wooden shacks. The railway features in some other walks.

Over the river follow the line of the railway to cross a stile directly ahead, continue along an enclosed path over a dyke, climb to the next stile and continue along the old track bed to a further stile beneath the overhead power lines. Over this leave the trackbed and climb the left-hand embankment, following the hedge until it meets a fence at a stile and seat. (760m)

The railway here entered its only cutting before joining the main line. In the cutting is one of the few exposures of the underlying rock—a wet, friable sandstone that serves as an aquifer. This area is now fenced and has been planted as a memorial nature reserve. A stile gives free access.

Over the stile go half right to pass the corner of the wood to reach a tall stile and gate, giving access to a track that carries you over the railway and motorway. (300m)

Note how the stream crosses the motorway before it is piped over the railway.

4

Continue along and up the track when it becomes a metalled lane. Immediately after the first farm on your left, Clarkson's, with its double gated yard, go over the stile by the gate to enter the field above the farm. Walk along the left-hand ditch, cross the concrete footbridge and turn right in the next field. Go along the right-hand boundary through a gate and continue ahead to the stone post stile by the metal gate, cross and continue along the right-hand boundary to a stile between the vicarage and Barnacre Church. Continue over the stile along an enclosed path to reach the road down a few steps. (1000m)

Barnacre Church organises an annual July church exhibition when all the members of this widely scattered parish display their talents on differing themes of local life. The stained glass windows of the church are of Northern saints. The church is another solid example of Paley and Austin's work, built in 1905 at the expense of the local landowner.

Walks A and B part here.

WALK A

GO RIGHT along the road to the junction and go through the field gate facing you or use the adjacent double stile arrangement. In the field follow the left-hand fence and wood to cross a stile. Follow the fence around the corner but turn right when a fence comes down the field and follow this fence up on your left to cross a further stile. Continue in the same direction alongside an old hedge line to a stile on the right of the pond in the top corner. (1000m)

Looking back from this hillside gives extensive views across the Fylde towards Blackpool—and it gives you a rest from your exertion.

Over this stile cross the narrow field ahead by walking parallel to the right-hand boundary to find and cross a further stile which gives access to a farm drive. Go left down the drive to Birk's Farm and continue on the lower branch of the track to pass straight through the gated farmyard, with the house and a stone barn to your left, to reach the last (a black corrugated iron) building on your left. (500m)

Go through the left-hand of four adjacent gates facing you, follow the track down through a gate by the stream and enter the next field. Leave the rough track on entering the field to climb the slight banking to your right. Then cross the field to a small gate some 50m above the far left-hand wood and gate in the corner of the field. (500m)

From this gate there is an extensive vista, from Blackpool, around Morecambe Bay to the fells of the Black Combe ridge. However the mass and bulk of Heysham nuclear power stations form a major blemish on the landscape.

Through the gate follow the left-hand fence to a stile and gate over which you follow the track down to Burn's Farm. Just past the house go left to enter the farmyard. (320m)

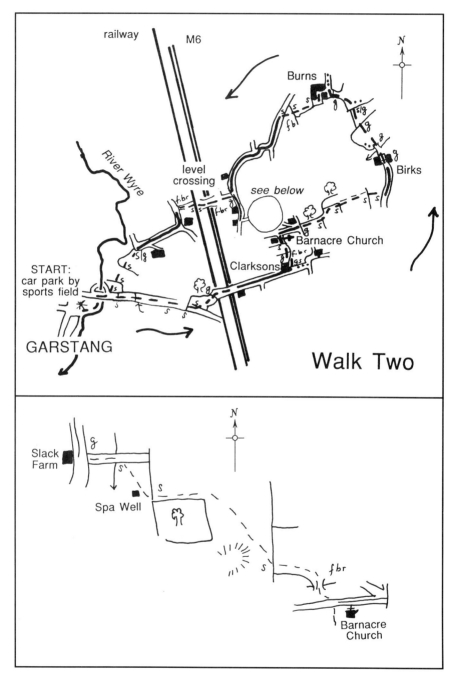

The refreshments at Burn's Farm are well recommended, but are available only on Wednesdays and at weekends.

To continue, go left again in the yard, with the portaloos to your left, and climb the stile just behind the last building on the right. In the field follow the left-hand boundary down to a stile facing you at the bottom corner of the field. Cross this stile and subsequent pole footbridge, go over the next small footbridge and then the following stile to reach the farm access road. (370m)

Go left down the road, right at the first junction and keep straight on when a road joins from the right. After the stone-built keeper's cottage on your right go to the third gate on your right (short of the white-faced cottage) and enter the field.

Here both routes rejoin. (900m)

WALK B

CROSS DIRECTLY over the road from the steps, descend more steps to cross a footbridge and in the field go left to climb by the left-hand boundary to a stile in the corner. Over go half right to cross the field to the right of the delph (old quarry) and reach the top corner of a wood where views of Lakes can be seen. Descend the steep side of the wood to a further stile. Over this go right by the fence to find Lady Hamilton's Well. (300m)

Hewitson describes.this as 'The Spa Well' where the Hamilton family used to bathe when they stayed at Woodacre Hall (the original is no longer extant). Lady Hamilton lived on in this area after her husband had died and perhaps it was her use of this spring-fed well, with its alleged medicinal properties, that has led to the well being more frequently named after her.

From the well cross the remainder of the field to a stile by the stream, go left up the track to emerge on the road opposite Slack Farm. Go right down the road, pass a cottage and then go left to re-enter the fields by a stile after the first fieldgate on the left after the cottage. (300m)

Walks A and B rejoin here.

Make down the field to cross the prominent footbridge over the motorway. Cross the next field to a stile and then cross the railway with GREAT CARE. In the next field follow the right-hand hedge down to a stiled footbridge and onto the road. Turn left along the road, but follow a track which goes off to the right when the road bends left. (600m)

Follow the track down, pass the junction and, when it bends right, cross the stile on the left between the two gates. Follow near the right-hand boundary and after 30 metres cross the field to a stile in the far fence and aiming towards the bridge over the river. Over the stile cross the next field in the same direction to a further stile. Continue to the stile by the embankment where you can recross the Wyre and return to the car park (1200m)

Mills on the Calder

Garstang—Calder Vale—Garstang

10 kilometres (6 miles)

Start: Garstang Community Centre Car Park (GR 493454)

O.S. Pathfinder map 668 (SD 44/54) Garstang

THIS WALK is mostly on field paths and tracks and encompasses aspects of industrial archaeology along with fine scenery—giving long distance views as well as passing through woodlands. The walk is superb at bluebell time but an all-year-round favourite for views of the Lancashire coast. The route is mostly on land owned by the Barnacre estate and a large number of their pheasants will be amongst the 'wild' life that crosses your path.

Follow the start of Walk 2 as far as the lane up to Clarkson's Farm, which you continue past to meet a road where it rounds a double bend. Go straight across to a concrete farm road on the right of the cottage. (2000m)

This house was the site of a wailing cross—where the coffin bearers could rest and the mourners could wail.

Follow the track over a cattle grid and up towards Heald Farm. Immediately short of the farmhouse enter the second wood on your left by a stile and cross the rough ground near to the left-hand boundary to a further stile and barrier gate in the top corner. Over this go left to leave the farm by a gate by the corrugated iron barn and enter a field ahead. (470m)

Turn right and follow the right-hand hedge up to the crest of the field. (250m)

This is the highest point of the walk. The views across the Fylde, to the Lake District and of the local Bowland fells can be very impressive.

After the stone posts continue to follow the beech-lined right-hand fence down, and cross over two stiles by gates to reach the next road. (240m)

Cross the road to the gates by the bungalow, go through the middle of three gates, follow the right-hand fence to cross a stile by a footpath sign. Then follow the ditch behind the bungalows to a stile in the field corner, cross, turn left and go to cross a footbridge. (200m)

Cross the field to a stile with one stone post some 15m right of the telegraph pole and then keep parallel to the right-hand buildings to a stile at the left-hand hedge of

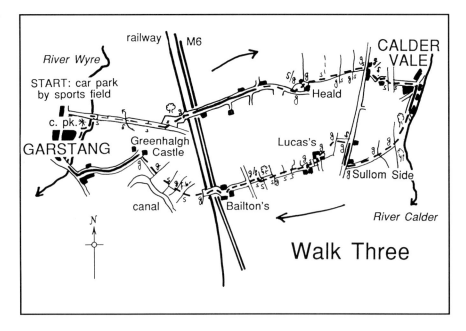

a small wood. Follow the wood-side enclosed path that continues behind some houses and then descends by steps to the road at Calder Vale. (375m)

Calder Vale is a most unexpected sight—an industrial village enveloped in the fold of the Bowland foothills. The stone architecture of the mill village is not without its charms. The mill was built as a four-storey cotton mill in 1835 with thick stone outer walls and cast-iron pillars. There are remains of the old mill race with the mill pond above the village. The waterwheel was replaced by a turbine; there was once a beam engine and, in 1909, a gas engine. The mill, now electrically driven, weaves Arab head 'scarves' for export. The mill and village were built by the Jackson family who were Quakers. The lack of a public house in the village, the family said, was because they did not wish to see 'ragged children'. While brothers Richard and Jonathan founded the cotton mill, brother John opened a paper mill upstream at Oakenclough.

Cross the road and turn right down Albert Terrace, keeping all the cottages to your left, follow the track down for some distance to the final terrace of cottages. (500m)

The track goes down through steep-sided woods that are carpeted in bluebells each May, and passes above the lodge of the village's other former mill (now demolished) and over the rocky bed of the River Calder to the twelve cottages and millowner's house of the former Barnacre weaving mill. This was opened in 1845 and was powered by waterwheel from water piped over the entrance arch. It later had a steam engine

9

whose chimney was built up the hillside. The single-storey mill stood just beyond the cottages.

Continue past the cottages and barrier until the track bends left. Leave by the sloping track that goes off to the right and climb through the woods to open fields reached by a gate. Follow the left-hand fence, go through the gate and then continue along the enclosed track which leads, eventually, down to the left-hand side of Sullom Side Farm and the road. (750m)

Go right along the road until you reach Walker House, the next cottage. Almost opposite the house is a gate and stile through which you follow the right-hand boundary down to another gate. Through this descend half left across the field to reach the yard of Lucas's Farm via a gate on the left of a caravan. (750m)

Go down the yard and left in front of the farmhouse and after 20 metres go right through a small gate in the hedge before the wood. Follow the wood-side down to a further (difficult) stile and enter the next field. Continue down the field aiming for a gate to the right of the farm buildings. Go through, turn right, go through the next gate and follow an enclosed track down into a field. The next stile to cross is in the bottom left-hand corner of the field by the ditch. (450m)

Continue along the left-hand boundary to a gate by the wood corner. Cross this and follow the woodside to a further stile, continuing over to a stile on your right at the end of the wood. Cross this and go left to reach a stile by a gate some 20 metres from the left-hand corner of the field. (250m)

Over the stile cross the road and go down the farm access track to pass through the gated, cobbled yard of Bailton's Farm, continuing to the right to cross the bridge over the motorway and railway. (550m)

At the first gate go through a tight gap stile on its right and cross the middle of the field to a further stile behind a lone oak tree standing proud of the hedgerow in the far, long side of the field. Over the stile cross the next field towards the right-hand pylon to reach a foot bridge and gate. Follow the left-hand boundary to cross a further stile with a plank footbridge beyond in the hedge that faces you. (470m)

(If instead you went left through the adjacent gate, then access could be gained to the canal towpath which could be followed back to Garstang.) (1500m)

Cross the next field aiming to the left of the farm buildings to a hedge and fence junction, each with a gate. Go through the right-hand gate and follow the left-hand hedge along to Greenhalgh Castle Farm. (475m)

Greenhalgh Castle Farm is a seventeenth-century building with stone mullioned windows. The stone was 'quarried' from the castle built in 1490 by the first earl of Derby, which was one of the last two strongholds in Lancashire to hold out against Parliament in the Civil War.

Go left down the metalled farm lane to reach Garstang. Over the bridge you can either walk up through the High Street or go by the riverside path that starts on the far side of the bus station, to the car park from which you began (1250m).

Fellside parish and ancient people

Garstang—Calder Vale—Bleasdale—
Brock Valley—Garstang (or Calder Vale)

22 kilometres (14 miles) from Garstang or 12 kilometres (7.5 miles)
from Calder Vale

Start: Garstang Community Centre Car Park (GR 493454) or
Calder Vale near the mill (GR 533458)
O.S. Pathfinder map 668 (SD 44/54) Garstang

FOR WALKERS who wish to start at Garstang then the first half of Walk 3 can be used to reach Calder Vale before going on to the remote and lightly populated parish of Bleasdale. From Garstang this forms one of the longer walks in this book. It can be undertaken at any time of the year (the boggy patches are always there!) but whenever you go it deserves a full day. Two stretches of road are used, the first being a private and quiet estate road that does not detract from the enjoyment of the walk. A short extension enables you to visit the pre-historic site of Bleasdale Circle.

Follow Walk 3 if you start at Garstang, and when you emerge at the road in Calder Vale go left down to the bridge over the River Calder with the mill on your right (4000m). The shorter walk starts here.

From here continue with the river on your left and pass Long Row cottages to find your path straight ahead at the end of the row where the road swings up and behind the cottages. The tarmacadamed path leads past the old mill pond, alongside the Calder, before climbing to the church and school. (800m)

Continue ahead to the road junction and go right to pass through a farmyard, and once through the gateway strike left up the field. Keep to the right of the old fenced quarry and climb a wall stile in the top right-hand corner of the field where the wall meets the fence. (500m)

Over the stile go left and follow the fence and streamlet, turn left when the fence bends left and go to the access track in front of Rough Moor Farmhouse. Carry on up the drive to the road and right on the road. After the bend in the road when it begins to descend, look for a wall gap on your left where a path leads through the short depth of trees and then, via a small gate, to the estate road beyond. (500m)

Turn right along the metalled estate road, pass through the gate by Fell End Farm and, after a further gate, arrive at the rear of Bleasdale Tower. (1250m)

Bleasdale Tower is the home of the Duckworth family and was built as a shooting lodge around 1840-50.

Keep straight ahead at the junction at Brook's Barn Farm and after the wooded section go left at the next junction to pass Brooks Farm and the bridge beyond over the infant River Brock. (750m)

Your bridge is one of three built by boys from the former local reformatory. Just upstream is a saddle (packhorse) bridge, which lay on the route from the villages of Hazelhurst (now a single estate farm) and Coolam to the wool towns of East Lancashire and Yorkshire. Hazelhurst had about seventy people employed in hand-loom weaving along with wool spinning. This once extensive village also had an ancient set of stocks. Coolam was said to be a community of felt hat makers but there is little evidence for this.

The metalled road then climbs and after a short distance the road bends right by a small wood. Go to the left along a short track to enter the fields by a gate. Follow the left-hand fence and arrive at Admarsh barn (note the 1720 date stone) and Admarsh Church by two further gates. (1000m)

To visit Bleasdale Circle go left while facing the church and follow the farm track to the cattle grid by Vicarage Farm, where permission to visit the circle can be given. Over the grid go right in the field and follow the boundary to cross a stile in the corner, then turn half right towards the circle site in the clump of trees. Retrace your steps to the church. (adds 1500m to walk)

Bleasdale Circle is centred on a small barrow whose graves contained two crema-tions in collared urns. There was also an incense cup. The circle consisted of eleven wooden posts (the remains of which are in the Harris Museum, Preston) and was bounded by a ditch and timber palisade. The diameter was nearly fifty metres. This unique woodhenge was dated to the Late Stone or Early Bronze Age. The positions of the wooden posts are marked by unseemly concrete pillars.

High up on the skyline from the opening to the circle is a man-made gouge in the skyline of Fairsnape Fell called 'Nicks Chair'. We wonder if it could have been an alignment with the circle ?

Admarsh or Bleasdale Church is a nineteenth-century construction with a 'quaint' Last Supper over the altar and two odd faces peering from carvings on old chairs. It is the only church dedicated to St Eadnor, who was possibly Eadbert who carried on Cuthbert's work at Lindisfarne and was buried in the saint's tomb.

With the church on your left go past the school and, just before the cattle grid, turn right at the road junction. (If you are in need of refreshment continue down the road to Bleasdale post office and after retrace you steps to the junction). (250m)

Follow this metalled lane until you reach a gate with stone gate posts, on your left amidst the beech hedge. Enter the field and go diagonally right to cross to a fence corner and continue in the same direction with the fence on your right. This leads to

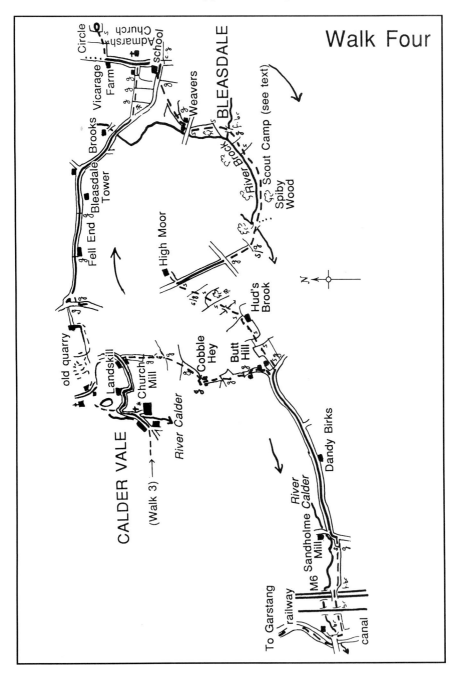

Walk Four

a gate and then, via a short enclosed track, to pass through the gated yard of Weavers Farm and on to the road. (750m)

Go diagonally right across the road, and climb the bank to cross a stile to enter the wood. Over the stile follow the path in the wood by the left-hand fence. Most people continue to follow the fence side path, but the actual right of way crosses the next stile on the left and follows the right-hand fence over two further stiles to a stile by the far corner of the wood. Cross the stile in the corner and go down the steep embankment near the right-hand fence and cross the small field to cross a footbridge just above the junction of the two River Brocks. (550m)

Keep the river now on your right and walk downstream to pass through a gate and continue in the same direction to cross a stile and enter the wood. From here keep on the distinct path near the river. Continue along until the path begins to rise by the toilet block of the Wood Top Scout Camp. (520m)

In the field below the main camp buildings go towards the river's edge and follow the paths near the river downstream, using the short up-and-downs to pass through the wood—the paths are very wet—and eventually reach Snape Rake Lane with a footbridge over the River Brock. (750m)

Maps name this as Boggy Wood—a very appropriate name. However the wood is being renamed Spiby Wood after the late Cyril Spiby of Preston, a rambler and guide book writer, as this was one of his favourite spots. A charitable trust has been set up, has leased the wood, and hopes to maintain the native deciduous character of the area and make the paths more easily walkable.

The sunken track, Snape Rake Lane, is actually a public road! Cross the footbridge and climb the track on the far bank. Go over the stile by the gate and follow the track between trees across the open field to reach the road at a T-junction. (500m)

Follow the Oakenclough road straight ahead and when you are just short of the access track to High Moor Farm on your right, cross the stile next to a footpath sign in the wall on your left. Cross the field towards the small wood using a wooden ladder stile by the gate to cross the first fence line. A stone stile, with a white marker post, admits you to the plantation and another takes you back into the fields after crossing this delightful area. (1000m)

Cross the field aiming above Hud's Brook Farm, crossing a small stream by a farm bridge in the field, and cross the stile with a white marker post in the boundary some forty metres above the farm buildings. Cross the next field, keeping parallel to the farm buildings and the wall on the left, to cross a stile with marker post. Another pair of stiles to be crossed is directly ahead. (300m)

Climb the short rise ahead and then cross one of the three stiles in your way. Drop down the field to the stile by the gate in the far right-hand corner and regain the road. (325m)

The people returning to Calder Vale go by a different route from those returning to Garstang. See later in this chapter for the way back to Calder Vale.

If you are returning to Garstang go right along the road and follow it right down for 2 kilometres until you reach a junction by Sandholme Mill, which was originally a three-storey corn mill and was constructed before 1841.

Turn left at the junction, cross the road and after 100 metres go right down a short enclosed track. When it ends go the stile between two adjacent gates and then follow the left-hand fence to reach and cross a prominent bridge over the motorway. (600m)

Over the bridge cross the field and go through the underpass bridge of the railway and in the next field go ahead by the left-hand fence, through a gate, and on to reach the canal side. Turn right to cross the River Calder, go left over the canal bridge and then down to the towpath. With the canal on your right it can be followed back to Garstang. (4000m)

The walk back along the towpath goes over Rennie's Wyre aqueduct. It is a particularly fine example of his building style, with sharply in-curved walls, and it is battered outwards to resist the pressure of the water.

If you are returning to Calder Vale turn right but go right again to the farm access track at Butt Hill Farm. Follow the track along to the left of the farm, pass Infield House and Sullom View on your left and continue until you reach the yard of Cobble Hey (note the datestone). (1000m)

A gate on the far side of the house enables you to leave the yard on a track that goes around by the right-hand wall to a gate in the far corner of the field. Through this gate continue directly ahead and go down towards a hollow where there is a gate to pass through. Continue up and round by the right-hand fence to reach the next gate. Through the gate a short enclosed lane leads to the two farms at Landskill. Go left in the gated yard and follow the metalled track down to Calder Vale. (1750m)

Landskill Farm is Jacobean, again note the date stone, with mullioned windows. Catholics once held their forbidden services here.

Above the edge of the Mosses

A: Garstang—Kirkland Hall—Nateby—Winmarleigh—Garstang

11.5 kilometres (7 miles)

B: as A going to Nateby Hall, but missing out Winmarleigh

7.5 kilometres (4.5 miles)

C: an even shorter alternative

6.5 kilometres (4 miles)

Start: St Thomas's Church, Garstang (GR 491451)

O.S. Pathfinder map 668 (SD 44/54) Garstang.

A N IDEAL CHOICE OF AMBLES around the parishes that skirt the western edge of Garstang. A few interesting buildings, a pleasant section of canal and with few contours to trouble the walker. An amble for a short, sunny, winter's day or a summer evening.

From St Thomas's Church go down Church Street to the canal. Go along the towpath, with the canal on your left, and when opposite the end of the basin, go right through a small gate and then cross the school playing field to pass through a kissing gate. (250m)

The path, called Many Pads, was probably the road to Churchtown, once the church for Garstang, and affords a view of Rennie's fine canal aqueduct.

Cross the next field to pass through the next kissing gate and then cross the next field to cross a stiled footbridge. As the path goes nearer to the Wyre bank, aim for the bungalow ahead to cross the field to a further stiled footbridge and then climb the bank to reach the A6 through a small gate. (750m)

Cross the A6 road to the left and at the end of the farm buildings turn right into the gated yard, go along the concrete track through the yard and then along the edge of the wood to two gates. Use the left-hand gate to enter a field and follow the track by the left-hand fence and ditch until it bends left at the end of the field. (700m)

Go through the gates facing you and then cross the next field directly to a gate and stile in the far right-hand corner near the rear of Kirkland Hall. Turn right on the track that starts over the stile and leads past the rear of the hall. Pass the front door of Keeper's Cottage, Kirkland Hall Farm and continue until the track bends left. (500m)

Kirkland Hall, once the home of the Butler family, has a seven-bay, two-and-a-half-storey brick façade built in 1760, but the wings behind contain some seventeenth-century brickwork and two datestones—1668 and 1695. The façade is better seen from Walk 6.

The Butlers were adherents to the House of Stuart and when the king's forces captured Kirkland Hall they took Alexander Butler and his servant, as prisoners, on horseback to Preston. However, on the journey the servant slipped from his horse and unseated his master into a ditch. The troopers came to his 'rescue' but found him more dead than alive and so left him to his fate. When they had gone he was remounted and returned home.

On the bend (Walk 6 continues down this road) go right to leave the road through the double field gate and into a field where you follow the track along the right-hand boundary and down to a double gate. Continue over the bridge (Ains Pool) and through the next double gate. Routes A and B depart from route C here. (250m)

Routes A and B

CONTINUE ACROSS THE FIELD that you have entered with the stone barn to your left and go almost parallel to the left-hand fence to cross a stile and footbridge in the farthest field boundary. Follow along the right-hand hedge of the next field, pass a lone hedgerow oak, until (just before a group of six consecutive hedgerow trees) a footbridge and stile on your right enable you to cross into the next field. (500m)

With your back to the stile go to the far top-left-hand corner of the field to cross a further stile and footbridge. In the next field follow the gappy hedge round to the right, pass the gateway and when the hedge gives way to fence cross this boundary. With your back to this gap go half left to cross the next field to a further stile in the far corner and to the right of a lone sycamore tree. (500m)

Over this stile follow the left-hand boundary to the farthest field corner and a stile. Over this stile go right and cross a further stile to gain access to the road. (400m)

Go left along the road and turn right into Kilcrash Lane. When this bends left leave the road by the stile facing you. In the field go to the left of the bungalow and then follow the right-hand hedge along to a concrete road via a stiled footbridge. Turn right on the road but leave it almost immediately by a stiled footbridge on the left and just before the gate. (700m)

Behind the farm is the Bowers, now a restaurant. The house is dated 1627 and one gable had a room with a clay floor that was used as a Roman Catholic chapel or oratory. There was talk of a secret passage from here to Nateby Hall, the next farm on our route.

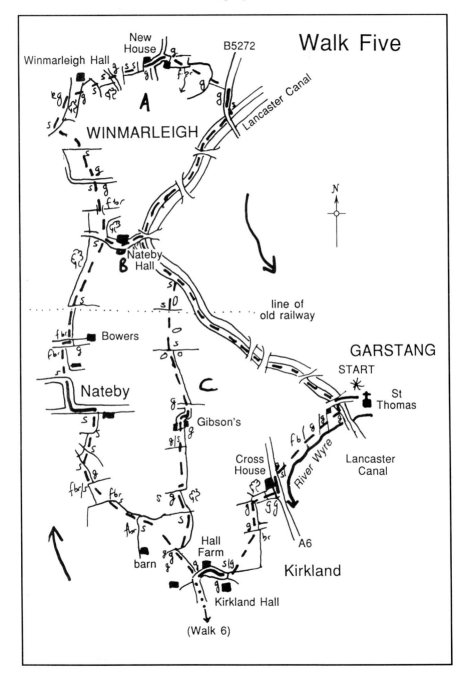

Winmarleigh Hall

New House

B5272

Walk Five

A

WINMARLEIGH

Lancaster Canal

N

Nateby Hall

B

line of old railway

Bowers

GARSTANG

START

St Thomas

Nateby

C

Gibson's

Cross House

Lancaster Canal

River Wyre

Hall Farm

A6

barn

Kirkland

Kirkland Hall

(Walk 6)

To the west and below our clay ridge lie the Fylde Mosslands—the only part of these still almost in their original state are the subject of Walk 8. The fields are more workable and productive than the grassy clay fields, although they can be just as wet.

Follow the right-hand boundary along through the field and, after a further stile, through a wood to a concrete stile. This is an old railway stile and the remains of the embankment can be seen on the left. Over the stile follow the left-hand boundary to the end of the wood after which cross the field by aiming for the trees to the left of Nateby Hall Farm. The hall from which the farmhouse gets its name was destroyed by fire in 1870. A stile and plank footbridge admit you to the track where routes A and B part company. (800m)

Route A

CONTINUE ACROSS THE TRACK into the next field and follow the right-hand fence alongside the trees until it bends right. Continue parallel to the left-hand boundary to cross to a footbridge beside an ash tree. Cross this and the next field aiming for Winmarleigh Hall, to reach a stile to the left of the wooden field gate, and the road. (470m)

Cross the road diagonally left to pass through a gate. In the field go parallel to the left-hand boundary along a slight hollow and cross the stile at the far end behind the hawthorns. Go half left to pass the triangular wood with horse jumps on your left and then cross the field to the left-hand end of the iron fence between the two woods and cross the stile. (370m)

In the next field turn right and follow the right-hand fence alongside the wood to reach a small swing gate in this boundary and directly opposite the farm. Go through the narrow wood using the swing gates at each end and emerge in the field where you continue parallel to the left-hand fence which crosses the front of Winmarleigh Hall, and cross the elaborate iron stile in the wooden fence across your way and to the left of a gate. (750m)

Winmarleigh Hall is part of the Lancashire College of Agriculture. It was built by Paley in 1871 for the Patten family from Warrington. The owner became the first and last Lord Winmarleigh—ill luck dogged the family. The house was four-storeys, of red brick with a cloister-like loggia. Partial rebuilding followed the fire of 1927.

Skirt the left-hand edge of the wood ahead and pass through the small gate in the far right-hand corner of the field. Cross the road, go through the gate and the next field, with Nicky Nook ahead. Cross the iron stile to the left of the gate in the fence ahead, and then follow the right-hand fence down over two stiles and through a gate into the yard of New House Farm to the road in front of the house. (250m)

Turn left on the road, but turn right down the first short farm access drive. In the left-hand corner of the drive go through the kissing gate (complete with tap!) beside the field gate to enter the fields. Go diagonally right over the field and cross the footbridge in the far right-hand corner and near an ash tree. Cross the middle of the next, diamond-shaped, field diagonally in the direction the footbridge points you, to reach a gateway on the left of an oak tree. Go through this gate, along the right-hand fence and through the next gate to reach the road. Turn right and go along to join the canal. Go right on the towpath, with the water on your left, back to Garstang (see final paragraph). (4250m)

Route B

THIS ROUTE turns right along the track, passes through the farm yard to a stile by a gate on the far end of the yard. Use this to enter the field, aim to pass the concrete stumps and gain the canal towpath by a stile opposite the top of the old lime kiln (see final paragraph). Follow the canal back to the start. (2250m)

Route C

THROUGH THE DOUBLE GATES turn right and follow by the pool side and along to the far corner of the field and cross the stile. Continue along the right-hand boundary, pass over the next (posh) stile by the gate and follow the track as it goes right along the wood edge. In the next corner bend left and continue along the farm track, via another gate and upmarket stile, all the way to Gibson's Farm. Pass through the gated yard and turn right for the farm access track to the road. (1300m)

Cross the road diagonally left and rejoin the fields through the gate. Go along the right-hand boundary and then cross the stile in the top right-hand corner. Cross the next field in the same direction to pass the left-hand edge of the fenced ponds in the remaining clumps of trees and then on to cross the shallow railway cutting and climb the next stile in the facing tall hedge. (600m)

In this last field before the canal go along the left-hand edge of the long, wooded pond and continue down to a stile that gives access to the canal towpath. Here routes A and B rejoin as you go right along the towpath back to your start. (2100m)

The canal towpath reveals two interesting signs of industrial archaeology, as well as wildlife. The first, just beyond Nateby Hall Bridge is an old limekiln—limestone from the Kendal area was brought and burnt to 'sweeten' the fields and make the clay easier to work. The remains of the bridge abutments of the former Garstang–Knott End railway are also passed on this stretch.

Churchtown and Myerscough

Garstang—Churchtown—Myerscough—Bilsborrow—Garstang

18 kilometres (11 miles)

Garstang to Bilsborrow only 10 K(6 miles)

Start: St Thomas's Church, Garstang (GR491451)

O.S. Pathfinder map 668 (SD44/54) Garstang

but with a short section on 679 (SD 43/53) Preston (North)

THIS SLIGHTLY LONGER ROUTE explores the somewhat flatter agricultural areas to the south west of Garstang. The scenery might not be as dramatic as earlier walks, but it has St Helen's Church, Churchtown and the College of Agriculture at Myerscough, coupled with views of the hills and a long stretch of canalside towpath where two of Rennie's aqueducts add to the charm. For those who find such a walk too long, then it could be shortened either by talking the bus from Garstang to Churchtown or by walking only to Bilsborrow and returning by bus, saving the canal section for another day.

Follow Walk 5 from St Thomas's Church as far as the access track at Kirkland Hall Farm. (2200m)

Continue along this track at the left-hand bend and along to reach the A586. Cross the road to the left and go down through the middle of the village, passing the market cross and Punchbowl Inn (where lunches are served) to reach St Helen's church. (900m)

The village effuses some of that 'olde worlde' charm that attracts tourists and townspeople. It is a conservation area, though some developments leave a little to be desired.

St Helen's claims the title 'Cathedral of the Fylde' and this large church, the original parish church of Garstang (St Thomas's at the start, was a chapel of ease), is full of interest. Some of the stonework is twelfth century, and the circular nature of the churchyard indicates it being a site of pagan worship in Anglo-Saxon times.

The interior has an elaborate carved pulpit of 1646, oak beams given by Henry IV from the nearby hunting forest of Myerscough, and rudely carved miserichords that came from Cockersands Abbey (Walk 9). The church tower dates from the fifteenth century and the yard contains some plague death gravestones and two, with carvings showing people in prayer, are referred to as 'Adam and Eve'.

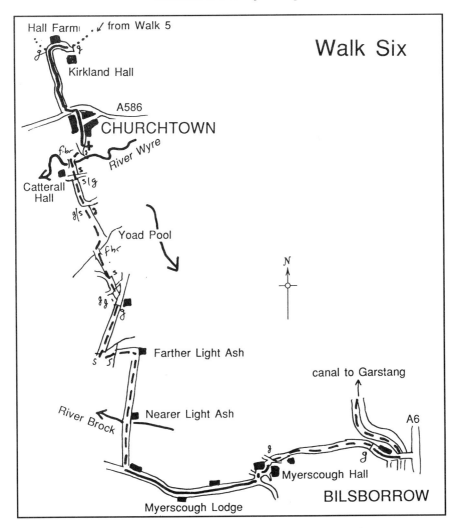

Walk Six

The river once lapped around the church and it has been suggested that the church owes it origins to Celtic missionaries who came up the river in coracles. A leaflet, available for sale in the church, gives details of a church and village trail.

From the rear of the church go through the small gate at the rear of the new graveyard and along above the river bank to cross the suspension footbridge to your right. The footbridge was opened in December 1985 to replace one washed away in the floods of 1980. The cost was £160,000. (200m)

On the far bank, with Catterall Hall Farm to your right, go by the left-hand hedge after crossing the stile, pass through the stone stile, and go over the stile by the gate facing you to follow the farm access track. Follow this enclosed track (which has varieties of daffodils blooming on either side in spring) until it bends left. (370m)

Go through the stone gap stile between the two gates facing you on the bend and follow the left-hand side of the field down to the bottom left-hand corner, turn to your right across the bottom of the field and go to cross a footbridge over the unusually named Yoad Pool in the far corner of the field. (450m)

Over the bridge follow the right-hand boundary until a stile enables you to cross it (if the stile is missing go through the iron gate that marks the line of an underground pipe). Over the stile go left to meet the farm track, continue along this and when a further track crosses your way continue straight ahead through two gates to reach a metalled road by a house. (400m)

Turn right at this junction, go through the wooden gate and follow the enclosed green lane down until it ends at a stile, which you cross. (500m)

Go left along the embankment, cross the next stile and then follow the left-hand fence towards Farther Light Ash farm buildings. Cut across to the right-hand side of the buildings to meet the access road. (300m)

Follow this road to the right, as it passes Nearer Light Ash Farm and crosses the River Brock to reach a metalled road. Go left on the road, pass Myerscough Lodge Farm on your right and, when the road bends right, leave it to the first left-hand driveway into Myerscough College grounds. (2350m)

Myerscough Hall was formerly the site of the house where King James I stayed when he enjoyed the hunt in Myerscough forest and the attached deer park. The hall also had a corn mill. On your way through the college grounds you will become aware of some of the many activities that take place at the college.

Go down the access drive with the woodland garden on your right, turn first right and go along to a T-junction of roads where you turn left. Follow this metalled road right and then left until it goes through a gate (signed to the pavilion). The track is now unmetalled, bends right, passes the college's equestrian centre and continues along as an enclosed track to Bilsborrow. (1370m)

When the track crosses the canal you can go down the steps to your right, go under the canal bridge with the canal to your right and walk the five miles back to Garstang. The way gives extensive views of the Bowland Fells, and watch for the blue flash of the kingfisher or the fishing herons. On the other hand go you can go ahead to the A6 and the bus stop to Garstang is just to your right. (8000m)

The Badger's river

Brock—Bleasdale—Claughton—Brock

21 kilometres (13 miles) but with shorter (14.5 kilometres) and longer alternatives

Start: The A6 road at Brock by the Dutton Forshaw Land Rover Garage
(GR 512406) just south of The Green Man. As well as the bus stopping here
cars can be parked on the bridge or by the level crossing.
O.S. Pathfinder map 668 (SD 44/54) Garstang

A S WITH OTHER ROUTES, we suggest a shorter version and, in this case, a slightly
longer route that returns to the start via the canal from Catterall.

The River Bock is one of the all time favourites of local ramblers, partly because
of the length of continuous path besides the river but mainly for the delightful scenery
and wildlife along the route. The lower river is one of dippers, wagtails and the
occasional kingfisher; the higher fields are the homes of curlew, wagtails and sandpi-
pers whilst the upper reaches are the preserve of pheasant. Many of the paths used
can be very wet and muddy—you have been warned.

Immediately south of the garage is a short track to the former Brock railway station
and level crossing. Cross the railway with the pedestrian traffic lights and then follow
the path towards the river, under the motorway and along the track to an aluminium
footbridge over the Brock which you cross. On the far bank go left along the bankside
track to meet the road at New Bridge and its weir. You will have to retrace your steps
along this section at the end of the walk. (1300m)

Cross the road directly to a gap stile and go to the riverward side of the revamped
buildings at Brockside. Cross the footbridge, go past the buildings, up a few steps
and over the stile. Go slightly right to cross the next stile by the gate. In the long
field follow the left-hand fence, which goes alongside the river, to cross a stile by a
gate at the far end. Note the small gorge and waterfall below to the left. (900m)

Use the stile to enter the next field and follow near the left-hand boundary to cross
the next stile by a gate. Continue by the left-hand fence to cross a stile by a gate and
then follow the rutted track by a line of trees to reach the road by a further stile by
a gate. (370m)

Go left over Walmsley Bridge—note the dates—and on the far bank go right over
a stile to re-enter the fields. Cross the field to avoid the sweep of the river. A stile
admits you to a path through a short wood. A further stile puts you back into the

riverside fields. Follow near the left-hand fence until the field narrows and then, through the gate, continue along the bankside path to another stile and gate across your way. Continue near the riverbank until an old hedgeline comes from your left. Follow this on your right away from the river, pass a short, redundant footbridge and up to a gate. (1100m)

Through the gate go right down a signposted track to pass the ruins of Brock Mill. The old corn mill ruins to the right still show the remains of the buildings but they are in a dangerous condition. The mill once produced files for the metalworkers.

The path continues straight ahead and meets the river near a footbridge, but do not cross it. From here to the picnic site and car park at Higher Brock Bridge the path continues near the riverside through some very attractive woodlands. Go to the road, cross the bridge and go through the gap stile by the gateway immediately on your left. (1500m)

Continue left past the former Brock Mill to a gate and stile which lead you into a field. Go by the right-hand fence and, when it bends right again, continue directly ahead to meet the left-hand fence by the river and on to reach a stile in the left-hand corner of the field. (200m)

Cross over the stile and follow the riverside path along to the Thirlmere Aqueduct that crosses over the river. Go right here to climb the embankment in the corner, cross the track to the cottage and go into the wood by a gap, once a stile, just below the aqueduct gate. The path now follows a fence line by the bottom of the wood and reemerges by the river's edge. Continue along the riverside path, with some very wet patches, to meet Snape Rake Lane, reputedly of ancient origins, and a footbridge over the river. (1000m)

For a short cut you can follow Walk 4 from here until it intersects with our route again. (1000m)

The next stretch is through the very wet Spiby, formerly Boggy, Wood (see Walk 4 for details). The path climbs to the left of Snape Rake, but several paths meander above the river and eventually go down to the riverbank which you continue to follow to Woodtop Scout Camp. Join the track near the toilet block and follow it to continue through the wood and re-enter the fields by a double stile just after the end of the track. (1100m)

Cross the field, parallel to the right-hand wood, to the next gate and continue by the left-hand fence in the second field towards the footbridge where the two branches of the River Brock join. Do not cross but go right to pass by some ruins of a former farmhouse at the foot of the wood. (450m)

Go along across a double stile and follow the wet path by the left-hand fence to a footbridge over a side stream of the Brock. Cross the bridge and climb the gently rising clough-side path to a stile and gate. Cross the stile and follow the line of old trees, with Parlick Pike ahead to a gate and stile. Over the stile follow the left-hand

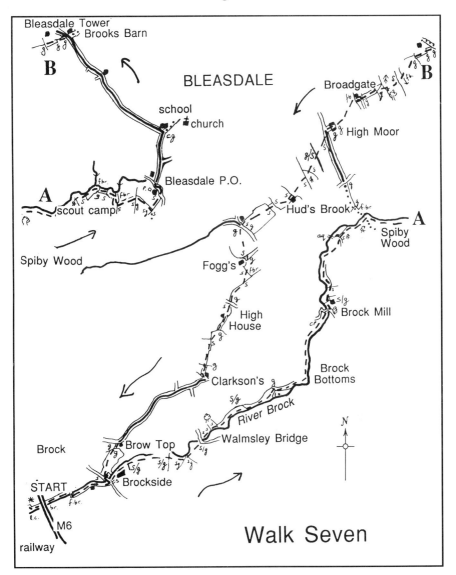

Walk Seven

fence to the far left-hand corner of the field. In the corner go over the left-hand stile on the nearside of the left-hand gate. In this next field follow the right-hand boundary down to a stile, some stone steps and the road. Go left down the road to Bleasdale Post Office where lunch and refreshments are available. (1000m)

To continue go past the post office, over the bridge and turn right through the gate on the Bleasdale Estate road. Keep left at the first branch and go immediately left over the cattle grid. Ahead of you lies Admarsh Church and, some distance beyond, Bleasdale Circle (see Walk 4 for details). (600m)

Go down the estate road, over the dip of the Brock by Brooks Farm and its saddle bridge (again see walk 4), continue on the road climbing up, ignoring the left turn until a road goes right at Brooks Barn Farm. (1700m)

Leave the road on the left by the second of two gates, go along a short track, through a gate, along the left-hand fence in a field below Bleasdale Tower, and through a further gate into a large field. Go half left down this field to find a stone footbridge and stile into the wood some 30 metres above the far corner of the field. (600m)

Follow the path through this small, rhododendron-infested wood, continue by the right-hand fence and leave by the stile facing you. In the field follow the right-hand fence round to the right of two adjacent gates. Through this gate go along the left-hand wall and fence and enter the yard of Broadgate Farm by a further gate. (500m)

Go between the first buildings, turn right into the yard and then immediately left to a small gate through which you pass the front door of the farmhouse to a further gate and small footbridge in the next field. Go half left up the next field aiming for the far left-hand corner of the farm buildings. (370m)

A series of gates takes you through the farm buildings and eventually down the access track to the road. Those taking the short cut via Walk 4 will rejoin here. (100m)

Cross the road diagonally left and go over the stone stile into a field. Cross the field towards the small wood using a wooden ladder stile by the gate to cross the first fence line. A stone stile, with a white-topped post, admits you to the plantation and one takes you back into the fields after crossing this delightful area. (500m)

Cross the field aiming above Hud's Brook Farm, crossing a small stream by a farm bridge in the field, and go to cross the stile in the boundary some 30 metres above the farm buildings. Cross the next field, keeping parallel to the farm buildings and the wall on the left, to a further stile. Another stile, of two, to be crossed is directly ahead. (500m)

Climb the slight rise directly ahead and then cross one of the three stiles in your way. Drop down the field to the stile by the gate in the far right-hand corner and regain the road. (370m)

A slightly longer route back to Brock would be to follow Walk 4 to the canal and go along the towpath, with the canal on your left, to bridge 47. From here a short walk down the A6 will return you to the start. This adds a couple of miles or so to your route.

To continue the main route cross the road and re-enter the fields by a stile by a gate. Go half left, pass the old tree, over the hummock and descend to a cross a stile by a gate across the farm track just under the overhead power cables and just above the farm buildings. Cross the next field by following the overhead cables to a footbridge and stile to the right of the pole-mounted transformer. The direction of a continuation of the overhead wires enables you to cross the next field to cross a further stile. Now follow the right-hand boundary to a gate which gives access to a road. (950m)

Cross the road and the facing stile and go up the field to the gate in middle of the long farm building (which in winter may be used as a shippon). Go forward and then left to pass through the yard of the seventeenth century High House Farm. Pass through the gate between buildings at the far side, go down the enclosed lane and through the gate at the end into the left-hand of two fields. (250m)

Climb up the middle of the field and cross the stile in the fence that crosses your way. Over, turn left, and follow the left-hand fence down to a gate in the bottom left-hand corner. A short track passes the old Clarkson's Farm and continues to the road. The road is followed right for about three-quarters of a mile—ignoring a left turn and a right turn until after a wood on your right, part of the Claughton Estate through which you have been walking for some distance, the road bends sharp right. (1900m)

On the left is the stone built Brow Top. Go through its gate, up the track through the former farm yard, through a long wooden gate at the top, across a small yard, and through a further, metal gate. The secret of this last field is not to climb so start off by going half right, but on meeting the right-hand boundary go partially left to come down the field to a stile in the corner by the right-hand side of the white house. Over here is the road and a few steps left take you over New Bridge and the riverside tracks back to Brock. (1750m)

Lancashire Mossland

Winmarleigh—Cockerham Moss—Winmarleigh Moss—Winmarleigh

12 kilometres (7.5 miles)

Start: by the Patten Arms on the B5272 Garstang to Cockerham road (GR 479491)

O.S. Pathfinder maps 668 (SD 44/54) Garstang and 659 (SD 45/55) Galgate and Dolphinholme

W ALKING ROUTES to the west of the A6 are neglected by walkers because they feel that a lack of contours means a lack of interest!

The last unreclaimed mosses represent what much of the Fylde of Lancashire must have looked like in times past although some drying out and the invasion of birch trees is changing this. The route across the moss, which should be a straight line, weaves in and out of rough ground and trees.

The mosses are of interest to naturalists largely because of the flora and insect fauna. This remnant of the lowland peat is now such a rare sight in Lancashire and of such importance for nature conservation that it has been declared a Site of Special Scientific Interest. This also means that the vegetation under foot is somewhat rough over the mossland.

Starting from the Patten Arms go along the road towards Cockerham, but soon turn down the first track off to the left. Go over the stile by the gate and follow this enclosed track until a gated, enclosed track enables you to turn off to the right. The track, like part of the next sections of path, looks towards Cockerham Church and, on a clear day, the Lakeland hills. (1000m)

Go along this track to reach the buildings of Lanthwaite Farm, pass the first building on your right, turn right to pass through the gated farmyard and leave by a gate adjacent to the farmhouse garden wall. A track leads to another gate and through this continues by a right-hand fence and down to pass through a gate. Through here continue down the left-hand hedge, ignore the gate, and when you come to the corner of the field, by the fenced dyke, turn right and follow the dyke along to cross a stile by a gate and a small footbridge in the next corner. (1900m)

Little Crookey Hall, last used as a special school, can be seen ahead. Built in 1874, it has been described by Pevsner as a 'medium sized mansion'.

Cross the next field to go over the gated stone bridge that crosses the River Cocker and go left through the next gate and alongside the riverbank. Continue through the

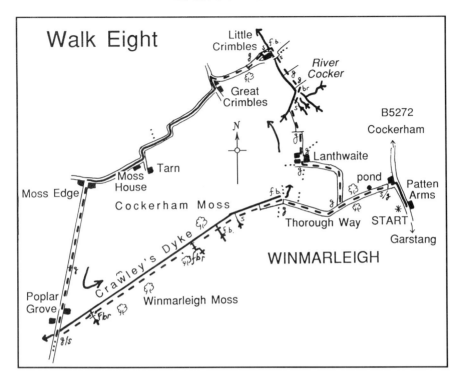

Walk Eight

Little Crimbles

River Cocker

Great Crimbles

B5272
Cockerham

Tarn

Moss House

Lanthwaite

pond

Patten Arms

Moss Edge

Cockerham Moss

Thorough Way

START

Garstang

WINMARLEIGH

Crawley's Dyke

Poplar Grove

Winmarleigh Moss

next gate and then to a stile by the farm access bridge. Ignore this bridge but re-cross the river by the next footbridge. Go over the stile and half left in the paddock, pass through the gate between the outbuildings and then turn right between the buildings in the yard of Little Crimbles Farm and follow the track round and eventually continue down the farm access road to the metalled road. (1350m)

From here until we leave the metalled road we are on the route of the Lancashire Coastal Way.

Turn left along the road and then right along the narrow Gulf Lane opposite the mullioned Great Crimbles farmhouse. The road is followed past the access to Tarn Farm, Moss House Farm and on to Moss Edge Farm on your left. (2250m)

At Moss Edge, with its large buildings and unsightly scrap, turn left between the barn and the Granary farm holiday cottage to follow an enclosed track that finally reaches Poplar Farm on the left. Continue past Poplar Grove on your right and then leave this track by the first gate and stile on the left. (950m)

Follow the left-hand boundary, cross the footbridge and enter Winmarleigh Moss. (300m)

The dyke on the left is called Crawley's Dyke. There is also a cross and a farm named after this person in the locality.

Proceed to cross the full length of the moss keeping as near to Crawley's Dyke, on your left, as the vegetation allows. Look out for plants and butterflies along your way. At the far end leave the moss by a further footbridge and re-enter the fields. (1450m)

In the field continue by the left-hand dyke and cross a footbridge, continue by the dyke to a stile on a bridge but with overhead power cables spoiling your view of the Bowland Fells ahead. (300m)

Over the stile continue along the left-hand dyke along to a stile near a gas pipe compound. Ahead lies Thorough Way which you follow to the start of your journey. (2500m)

The name Thorough Way appears to give the route an air of pre-history. Its use, and possibly its origins, lie in the removal of peat moss as litter for poultry houses around the turn of the century when two extraction companies were involved.

Of water and abbots

Cockerham—Bay Horse—Glasson Dock—Cockerham

16 kilometres (10 miles) or

Cockerham—Glasson Dock—Cockerham

13 kilometres (8 miles)

Start: Cockerham Parish Hall (GR 465521)—bus passengers might be better starting from Bay Horse on the A6 between Preston and Lancaster
O.S. Pathfinder map 659 (SD 45/55) Galgate and Dolphinholme

Main Route

The walk is of great interest—the best of the Lancaster Canal, Glasson Dock and Cockersands Abbey being the main highlights. Those opting for the shorter route will pass Thurnham Hall but miss much of the canal. This is a walk not to be underestimated for its variety of scenery. This walk includes a section of the Lancashire Coastal Way.

From the parish hall go towards the village centre and on your right find a path alongside the near end of cottage number 27. Go through the garden and over the stile at the rear, pass the barn, go through the gate and follow the right-hand hedge over the hillock. (170m)

From this drumlin there are extensive views of Wyresdale, the Lakes, Morecambe Bay and towards Winter Hill in the south.

When the hedge juts slightly into the field a double stile enables you to cross and follow the hedge now on your left. The next stile to cross is in the hedge that crosses your way some 10 metres from the corner, then cross the next field to reach the right-hand side of a wood and a gate. Through this, go left to pass through the next gate and then aim for the left-hand side of the wood ahead to reach a footbridge, and cross the River Cocker. (700m)

Follow up the edge of the wood, pass through a gateway and follow the right-hand hedge up the field to the top right-hand corner. Go through the gate on the right and then through the one on your immediate left. Cross this last field on this section to a gate at the rear of Centre Farm ahead. (450m)

Through the gate cross the track to follow the track ahead with the farm buildings to your right. This enclosed track becomes metalled at Holly House Farm and then leads you down to the canal. (1100m)

The canal is followed northwards, with the water on your right, and when it comes to a high arched bridge over the Glasson Branch cross and turn down left to follow the seven-locked branch some 4.4 kilometres to Glasson Dock. (6400m)

The canal stretch has wooded sections, a rock cutting through the local sandstone (also seen on the coast by Cockersands Abbey), an attractive junction and the locks and wildlife along the way to Glasson. The branch was opened in 1826 and, in common with the Leeds–Liverpool and Lancaster canals, has tall wooden footbridges and side weirs of the locks.

The parent Lancaster Canal runs between the 50- and 100-foot contours and was built following a 1792 Act of Parliament. Its main uses were both industrial and agricultural as well as for passengers. It carried coal from Wigan towards Kendal and limestone to the south. The first locks north are at Tewitfield on the now unusable section. The bridges are typical Rennie with a marked hump and strongly bowed with a true semi-arch.

Ellel Church, a private chapel of Ellel Grange, has a richly carved stone pulpit, and a coloured nave roof depicting apostles and evangelists is now in a state of disrepair. Ellel Grange was once the home of the Sandeman family (of port fame) but became a health farm and is now a Christian Centre. The house has a teetotal covenant tied to it.

Thurnham Mill, passed on the canal, was a water powered corn mill driven by turbine with a drying kiln on the north side. Water was taken from the canal, where the race can still be seen, but originally came from the River Conder. In more recent times it was a cattle feed mill. Now it is a public house with dining facilities.

Glasson Dock is largely a product of the canal age and developed when problems of silting in the Lune prevented ships from reaching St George's Quay in Lancaster. The main dock was constructed, after two Acts of Parliament of 1738 and 1749, to be large enough to hold twenty-five large merchant ships. Construction was completed in 1791 and later it was joined with the canal basin.

Much of its early trade was with the West Indies, whilst the first boat, the Sprightly of Duddon, sailed with slates from Furness to Preston on the opening of the canal link. The railway link with Lancaster (see walk 13) soon took away the canal trade. Even today it is a busy port but still attractive as a small tourist centre.

This part of the walk follows a section of the Lancashire Coastal Way which is well signposted. From the lock bridge in Glasson follow the road up Tithebarn Hill (which has a viewpoint indicator and with particularly fine views of Sunderland Point and the Lune estuary), keep left at the top and, at the next crossroads, near a farm with twin tower silos, go right down an enclosed lane to a pass through a gate beyond the caravan site. (550m)

Walk Nine

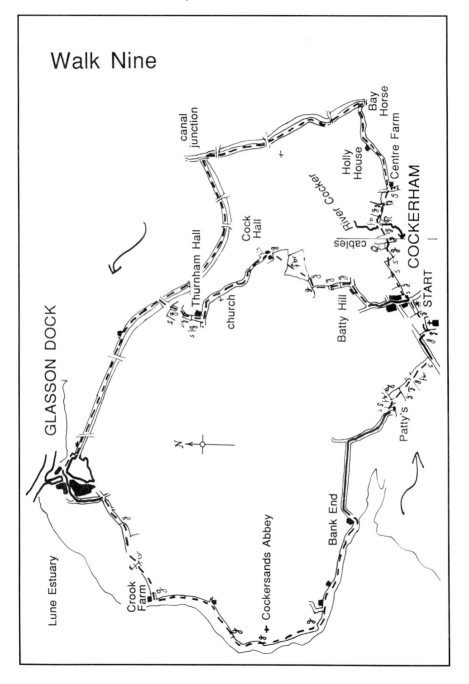

In the field follow the track by the right-hand hedge but then bending left to pass over a gated bridge and then follow a further hedgerow along to the rear of Crook Farm. Go through the gate to the left of the buildings and follow the farm access road to the left and along by the Lune Estuary. (1500m)

The area of the Lune and Cocker estuaries is a bird sanctuary and in winter with the tide well in provides a spectacle of many thousands of sea birds, particularly the waders.

Continue along the shore edge when the main access road bends left by the unusual lighthouse and house. Follow the embankment top path after the kissing gate by a gate and continue above the shore, passing Cockersand Abbey, to descend, after a further gate, a ramp to the shore. (2100m)

Cockersand Abbey, much neglected, was established by the Premonstratensians in 1190 at the site of a hospital built a decade earlier. It was the abode of hermit Hugh Garth before it became a colony for lepers and the infirm. The chapter house (c.1230), which remains, was a burial chamber for the Dalton's of Thurnham—its vaulted roof held by clustered columns with leafy capitals. The Daltons were probably responsible for the crenellation. The dissolution came in 1539 when the house contained '22 priests, five aged and infirm men "kept dayle of charitie", and 57 servants'. The church was without an aisle. An information board displays further details.

Continue along the foreshore, pass the ruined buildings, road end and Cockerham Sands caravan site, and on to reach a tarred road at Bank End Farm. Go ahead to follow the road beside the embankment, turn right at the junction at the far end, and continue along towards Pattys Farm and the parachute centre. Just before the final right-hand bend before the farm go left up the first of two pairs of steps up the embankment. (2250m)

This is where we leave the Lancashire Coastal Path but this route could be used to Pattys Farm where the road bends into the farmyard. To do so leave the road here and join the embankment immediately beyond the house. Follow this along to eventually reach the road which, followed to the left, goes to Cockerham.

Our route continues by climbing the stile on top of the embankment, where you go half right in the field to cross a stile and subsequent footbridge and then go through the gate in line with Cockerham Church with the parachute centre to your right. Continue directly ahead to the next gate and through follow the left-hand dyke—ignoring any access bridges that cross it—along through a gate, over two footbridges, (over a stile in a temporary fence) and over a stile in the far left-hand field corner that gives access to the road. (800m)

Go left along the road and then pass through the white kissing gate to follow a path that leads by the church and then follow the church access track back to the start. (300m)

Cockerham Church was rebuilt in 1910 by Austen and Paley. There are some plague gravestones.

Shorter Route

FROM THE VILLAGE HALL car park walk towards the centre of the village, bear right down the A588 at the junction by the pub and after the pavement ends continue down the road, and just after Batty Hill Cottage go right down the track to reach Batty Hill Farm. Go through the yard and immediately after the front of the farm house take the left-hand branch of the track and go down the enclosed lane, through a gateway and follow the right-hand hedge through the field. (800m)

The track continues straight through two fields and after the third gate in the far right-hand field corner turn right to continue to follow the track through two gates and along to pass through a further gate and enter a field. Bear left in the field and cross it slightly upwards towards the farm on the hillock with a pylon behind. (600m)

Aim for the farm, and the hedge across your way has a small footbridge in it. Over the footbridge go to the top right-hand corner of the farm buildings and pass through the left of two tracks to pass through the yard, keeping the farmhouse on your right. (100m)

From Cock Hall Farm follow the access track along, pass the Roman Catholic church and continue to the cattle grid over which you turn right and pass the front of the hall. (1150m)

The remote Thurnham Roman Catholic Church with its Egyptian-style tomb, the burial place of some of the previous owners of Thurnham Hall, is worth a few minutes of your time if the door is open.

Thurnham Hall, not seen from the main route, was once the home of the Dalton family (who were descended from Sir Thomas More), and was originally a thirteenth-century pele tower and the centre of a 50,000 acre estate. In the sixteenth century it was built to look like a small castle and it acquired a new front and chapel in the nineteenth century. In the wall is a 300-year-old vow, likely brought from Aldcliffe Hall, 'We are Catholic virgins who scorn to change with the times': the vow of two of Dalton's eleven sisters during Protestant rule. The house, with its attractive façade, is due to begin a new life with a commercial use—as a timeshare holiday home.

Go down the track with the hall to your right, through a gate and through a second gate, by the outbuildings, and enter the field. Go half right in the field on the track but after 15 metres turn left and cross the narrowest part of the field to follow an old enclosed track which you follow up to a stile and gate. In the field beyond the gate cross to reach the canal bridge from which you can descend with care to the towpath, short of the stile and gate, on the far left-hand side. You have joined the main route here. Go down the canal, with the water on your left, to Thurnham Mill and Glasson Dock. (2750m)

Middle Wyresdale

Scorton Picnic Site—Dolphinholme—
Street—Scorton

9 kilometres (5.5 miles) but a shorter alternative of 6 kilometres,
missing out Dolphinholme, is available.

Start: Scorton Picnic Site, signposted from Scorton village (1 mile to north of
village off the Trough of Bowland Road) (GR 504504). O.S. Pathfinder map 659
(SD 45/55) Galgate and Dolphinholme

A ROUTE THAT EXPLORES the middle reaches of the River Wyre. Old corn and
woollen mills offer industrial archaeological interest, whilst restored sand and
gravel extractions contrast a more modern industry with possibilities for the future
landscape of the dale. Observers of natural history should not be disappointed if they
keep a watchful eye. A good spring-time walk especially at snowdrop or bluebell time.

Leave the car park entrance and turn right along the road to cross the bridge over
the River Wyre. On the far wooded bank turn right along the bankside path, keeping
right at the arrow, until the path comes to a stile that leads into a field. (750m)

Cross the stile to enter the field and follow the dyke, a former mill race, along
towards the motorway where you turn left, cross the dyke and follow the right-hand
fence up and cross the footbridge over the motorway. The bridge, near the service
station, gives elevated views into upper Wyresdale. (500m)

In the field, cross towards the black corrugated iron barn of the farm to find a stile
to cross in the fence across your way, and in the next field go through the gate that
gives access to the farmyard. Go left down the farm access track and right at the
junction towards Guys—now a Girl Guide outdoor centre. A stone lintel in the barn
records the year 1633. (330m)

Go past the house and barn, through the gate into the car park, and turn left by
the edge of the buildings to pass through a small gate. Continue along the right-hand
hedge to cross a stile in the far right-hand corner and enter Duchy of Lancaster land
with well signposted paths. (100m)

In the field walk directly ahead towards the stone house, Sunny Side, and meet
the right-hand hedge by a stone slab footbridge and adjacent stile which you cross.
In the next field go left to a gate on the right of the beech hedge in front of Sunny
Side. Turn right through the car park and cross the two consecutive stiles to the left

38

of a gate. Follow the track through the gate, ignore the right turn and continue towards the wood. Continue along the fence with the lake on the left and cross into the riverside Fox's Wood when you meet the stile in the right-hand fence. Over this go left to a further stile and, over this, follow between the fence and river to emerge on the road by a further stile adjacent to Street Bridge. (1150m)

A shorter route goes right over the bridge and picks up our return route some 60 metres along by the gate marked 'private'.

Your way goes left along the road, but when it bends left go over the right-hand iron stile, hidden in the hedge, and go down to the riverside. Continue upstream, past the sadly neglected bridge that once gave access to Wyreside Hall, and up to a small gate into the riverside wood. (500m)

Wyreside Hall, dated 1852, with its dark grey stone and giant pilaster and porch of fluted Ionic columns is well placed to enjoy views of middle Wyresdale.

Use the path through the short wood and after the far gate turn right down to Corless Mill Farm. (250m)

Corless Mill, an old corn mill, displays a curiously roofed and shaped cottage—the first on your left before the farm—some, but not all, good examples of modern farm buildings, two millstones and the seventeen-foot diameter, five-foot wide water wheel. The mill house has gothic windows.

Continue past the farmhouse, through the small gate, and then cross the field to the far left-hand corner by the wood. Go over the stile and follow the woodside path to the road in Lower Dolphinholme. Turn right to cross the river. (700m)

The building first passed is the mill's 1797 warehouse now tastefully converted into houses. The mill itself was over the bridge and was built around 1787 as a worsted mill. It employed a thousand spinners with combing of the wool taking place in the houses. The single-aisled stone building on your right is a good example of an early traditional structure. The mill pond was over the road where a smaller part of the mill once stood.

The mill was one of the first to have a gas installation—the gas holder foundations are below the mill in the garden of the house—and was the site of an early experiment in taking the smoke underground to a double chimney we shall shortly pass. The mill was later used as a cotton mill but the distance from the railway made it uneconomic. It closed in 1868. However notice the restored gas lamp on the corner of the house when you cross the bridge.

Continue up the road and when it bends left cross the stile on your right (between two gates and signed to Wagon Road) and follow up the enclosed path through the wood to re-enter the fields by a curious iron ladder stile. The double mill chimney is to your left. (250m)

In the field gradually go away from the right-hand boundary and when a stone building appears in view use this as a guide to reach the stile you cross at the furthest

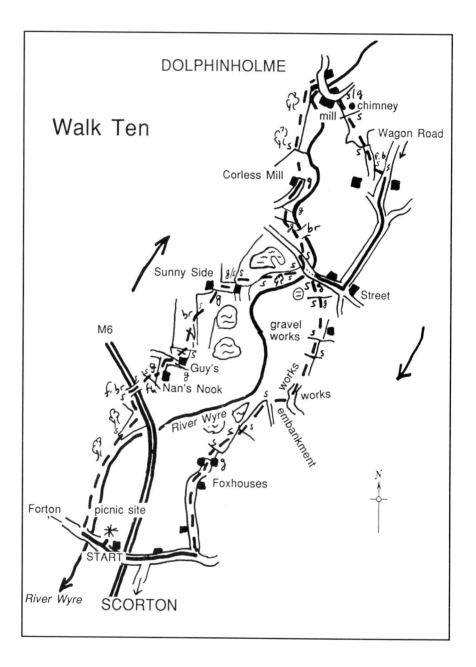

DOLPHINHOLME

Walk Ten

chimney

mill

Wagon Road

Corless Mill

Sunny Side

Street

gravel works

M6

Guy's

Nan's Nook

River Wyre

works

works

embankment

Foxhouses

Forton   picnic site

START

River Wyre   SCORTON

N

extremity of the field. Follow the enclosed path in the wooded area to the rear of Wyreside Hall and at the old kissing gate cross the stile on your left. In the field go half right towards the walled garden of the house to reach the road by a stile and small bridge. (600m)

This is Wagon Road, the connection between Dolphinholme and Leeds, Bradford and Norfolk for the long wagons carrying raw materials and finished yarns from the mill.

Go right down the road, right at the junction and right again at the cross roads to descend towards Street Bridge. Some 60 metres short of the bridge is a gate marked 'private' on your left. A stile and footbridge enable you to reach the rear of the gate. With the former gravel pit ahead turn left, cross the stile and continue to cross the next stile by the gate. (1100m)

Cross the next field by keeping to the lower part of the land and pass by the redundant stile on the left of the hedge, continuing along by the left-hand fence to a stile in the far left-hand corner of the field. (375m)

Over this stile go up the embankment—observing the warning signs by the settlement lagoons—and go left to eventually reach a track. Bear left up the track, cross the stream and enter the flatter area of the former sand and gravel working processing site. *Please note that at the time of writing this area is being reclaimed and waymarked changes to the path should be observed.* (500m)

Like many other river valleys with a shallow profile, the River Wyre has over the last few thousand years dropped some of its sediment load as silt, sand and gravel. These last two commodities are much in demand and thus the Wyre has suffered much in the extraction of these natural resources. The deposits are below the water table and thus the extraction process leaves lakes. These can be suitably graded and screened to become assets in the landscape and for fishermen and for wildlife. Certainly, the extraction phase is unsightly and disruptive, but the eventual mature landscape, if footpaths are left intact, can add new and acceptable features at the cost of the loss of some farmland.

Cross the flatter area to reach the far right-hand corner, pass the embankment end and turn left through the wooded area to reach a field corner. Re-enter the fields by a stile between two old gate posts. In the first field go along near the right-hand boundary to cross a stile in the far right-hand corner. In the next field follow the left-hand hedge to a further stile. Cross this stile and then go through the buildings at the rear of Foxhouse's Farm. (500m)

Follow the farm access road all the way to the road, go right and right again at the junction to cross over the motorway and regain the picnic site. (1500m)

Once an Abbot's home

Abbeystead—Hawthornthwaite—Catshaw—
Christ Church—Abbeystead

7 kilometres (4.5 miles)—although it is possible to take shorter routes

Start: Stoops Bridge, Abbeystead—to the east of the school where cars can be
parked by the river (GR 563543)

O.S. Pathfinder map 659 (SD 45/55) Galgate and Dolphinholme

A SUPERB SHORT WALK around Upper Wyresdale amongst fields and woods on each bank of the steep-sided River Wyre. The estate of the Duke of Westminster covers all this walk and the following route. The walker seeking a more strenuous route may wish to combine this with Walk 12. This walk, suitable for any time of the year, visits the shepherds' church and the lake and dam of Abbeystead reservoir, by the site of the 1984 disaster.

Abbeystead is named after the Cistercian abbey that was established here, possibly near where the two River Wyres join, by monks from Furness Abbey. The abbey existed only for a short period at the end of the twelfth century before the monks moved over to Ireland.

Camden describes the scene here as 'solitary and dismal'—solitary certainly but never dismal.

From the parking space by Stoops Bridge and the river bank of the Tarnbrook Wyre follow the road with the river on your right until it crosses a bridge over the Marshaw Wyre. (230m)

Just below the bridge the Marshaw and Tarnbrook Wyres join forces to carry their waters from the Bowland Fells down to the sea in Morecambe Bay.

Immediately over the bridge go right through an old gateway and down a few steps to follow the path through the woods. After a couple of small footbridges climb the bluff to the left by a series of stone steps. On top bear right to cross a stile and then follow the right-hand fence and cross the next stile. (300m)

In the field go left and follow the left-hand fence along, around a depression and then go through the left-hand of two gates. In the next field also go to the left-hand of two gates and then along the right-hand boundary to pass the front door of Hawthornthwaite Farm (although arrows waymark a route that bypasses the farm by going down to the left and around the farm by the road below the left-hand gate). Go

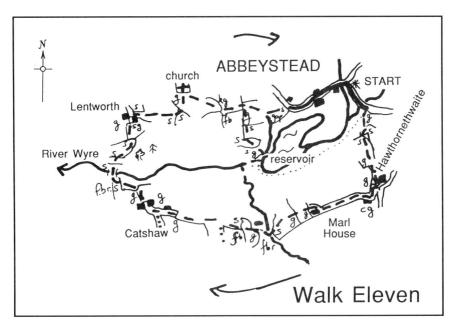

right on the track after the house and climb towards the barns, go right over the cattle grid on the nearside of the buildings and follow the track along to Marl House Farm. (1150m)

Along this track are extensive views of the upper amphitheatre of the Wyre. Abbeystead House, the shooting lodge of the Duke of Westminster, can be seen in its riverside setting amidst the trees.

Go to the right of the farmhouse, along the track to pass through the gate at the end and the one beyond. In the field cross to the gate and pass into the next field where you continue parallel to the left-hand fence and eventually down to a stile and footbridge over Cam Clough. (370m)

The rocks of the bed of Cam Clough show the wonderful carving action of the down-rushing stream. The smoothness, texture and shape are worth pausing to see.

Climb the steps and follow the embankment to the right until it curves and ends by some ruined buildings. (100m)

The embankment on which you have walked was the bank of a small reservoir that served the buildings, a former cotton spinning mill, with water power. The mill burned down in the mid-nineteenth century. Note the associated cottage ruins.

Climb the bluff with the mill buildings to your immediate right to find a small gate in the fence that gives you access to the field. Cross the narrow field directly ahead to a footbridge, stone steps and stile which lead you into a further field. (200m)

Follow near the left-hand fence and then continue in the same direction along the farm track to pass, via a gate, Little Catshaw Farm (1763), and then bear right to go into the yard of Catshaw Hall (1678). (820m)

The hall, now a farmhouse, is an ancient manorial residence and, like Hawthornthwaite, was listed in 1324 as a vaccary (cattle farm). The building is of great charm and vernacular interest and still contains some ancient woodwork—a black oak staircase thought to be as old as the house.

A gate, facing you across the yard, leads out into the fields where you go straight down by the old left-hand hedgerow to a gated depression. Through the gate the old track leads down towards the river but meets a fence from the left. Go over the stile in the fence and cross the footbridge over Hall Gill (a fairly uncommon use of the Norse name for a watercourse in this part of the world). The path over the footbridge continues along and then down right to the large footbridge, Long Bridge, over the Wyre. (600m)

People with the Pathfinder map may wish to make a short cut to the reservoir by following along the path near the river, but will miss the shepherds' church.

Whilst by the Wyre look out for the flying white blob, or the bobbing rock-perched bird, the dipper. The yellow wagtail or the flashing blue iridescence of the kingfisher may be spotted.

From the footbridge cross the narrow field to the stile, climb the steps through the wood, and leave by the stile at the top. In the field cross the track and follow near the right-hand fence as it climbs to a stile, which you cross, in the top right-hand corner and arrive at a seat. Follow the left-hand fence to a stile at the rear of Lentworth House Farm and after passing through the next two gates you emerge on the track by the farmhouse. (600m)

Opposite the end of the house, to your right, cross over the first of two stiles and follow the left-hand wall until it bends away. When it does so continue in your original direction across this flat field, aiming for the grey barns ahead, until at the far end the field dips down to enable you to cross two consecutive stiles and a footbridge. Climb the field to enter the churchyard by the small gate. (500m)

Christ Church is the shepherds' church. It sits high above the Wyre with its gargoyled water spouts leaning out from the squat tower of local stone.

The church site dates back to the fourteenth century and possibly earlier. It was rebuilt in 1733, and when the estate passed into the Sefton family it was extended. The pulpit dates from 1684.

On entering the church porch you will see wooden bars with iron hooks where the shepherds hung their crooks and lanterns. Note the inscription over the door. The windows date from the turn of the century and represent biblical shepherd scenes but set in local scenery. On display is a 'Geneva' Bible of 1599, so called because it was translated in that city during the times of persecution in England in the reign of Mary Tudor. It is sometimes called the 'Breeches Bible' because of Genesis 3 verse 7 stating that Adam and Eve made themselves 'breeches'.

Just above is the vicarage (where access to the church may be sought if the building is locked), a 1971 replacement of the 1733 building that still stands to the north, is the Sunday School built above a public stable.

From the small gate at the rear of the churchyard, the one you entered, go half left down the field, again aiming for the grey-roofed farm buildings, to pass through a small gate and footbridge in the far corner of the field. Climb up from the stream and go left along the old hedge to a gate, still aiming toward the grey barns. (210m)

If you want to take a short cut to omit the reservoir go through this gate and cut across the field to meet a concrete road below the right-hand corner of the lowest buildings in the field. Cross the track, go through the old gateway and then cross the field to a stile in the far right-hand corner near the house. Follow the road down right, pass through the hamlet and you come to Stoops Bridge. (900m)

For the full route go through the gate and turn right to follow the right-hand fence along to cross a further stile. Over this stile continue in the same direction to meet a stile that admits you to the top of the wood. Go left and down the wood and leave by a stile to join the concrete road. (370m)

Go right along the road and when it nears the stone wall on your left leave it to go through the small gate by the stone stile. Go towards the footbridge but turn left on the path that goes to reach the left-hand top side of the dam. However, despite the warning notices, it may be tempting to cross the fish pass and go down to the bottom of the dam and then continue around near the beautiful spillway and across the top of the dam. (150m)

The structure near where you leave the road is the end of the underground pipeline that brings water from the River Lune to flow down the Wyre before being abstracted lower down for people in South Lancashire.

The spillway of the dam is alive with glittering water, the fish pass reflects the clean state of the river whilst the reservoir above, now more like a natural lake, harbours bird life.

From the top left-hand corner of the dam the path goes up to a gate through which you continue by the left-hand wall and fence to reach the concrete road by a cattle grid. Go over the grid and continue up the road. When it has crossed a second cattle grid continue until you are level with the first barn on your left, where the short cut rejoins. Turn right off the track, go through the old gateway and then cross the field to a stile in the far right-hand corner near the house. (650m)

Follow the road down right, pass through the hamlet and you come to Stoops Bridge. (500m)

During the life of this book a new, permissive path may be opened from the footbridge below the reservoir dam and will return you to your starting point. If this path has been officially opened then cross the footbridge and go immediately left through a small gate (currently signed no admittance by the water authority) and follow the path up beside the river towards the top of the spillway. From here a wet and rough path follows, with water on the left and a wall (later a fence) to reach the path and road where you started out.

The twin rivers

Abbeystead—Tarnbrook—Marshaw—Abbeystead

10 kilometres (6 miles)

Start: Stoops Bridge, Abbeystead (east of school) (GR 563543)

O.S. Pathfinder maps 659 (SD 45/55) Galgate and Dolphinholme with a short section on 660 (SD 65/75) Slaidburn and The Forest of Bowland

THE RIVER WYRE begins its course on the fells above Abbeystead, and is formed from two main tributaries, the Marshaw and the Tarnbrook Wyres. This walk explores the dales of these two feeders. The whole of the catchment area is within the ownership of the Duke of Westminster and is managed for shooting and agriculture. The moors are said to be the best grouse shoot in England and the copse-speckled fields are managed for pheasant. The latter type of landscape predominates on the walk but extensive moorland views are gained.

Abbeystead House and its attractive gardens are seen from the path towards the end of the route. The area was once part of a royal hunting chase.

From Stoops Bridge go up the road that passes the entrance lodge to Abbeystead House and then climbs steeply uphill. When the road bends left leave by the front of the cottage on your right and go into the field behind by a stile at the rear of the garage and garden after passing through the garden. (500m)

Follow the right-hand wall and wood until it gently curves away to the right. Cross the remainder of the field by going under the overhead wires and aiming for the farm buildings ahead. Go through the right of two gates and follow near the left-hand fence and when a pole-mounted transformer and stone gate post are reached continue to cross the next field to reach the road over the stile to the left of the stone cottage ahead. (800m)

Cross the road and go down the short access track towards Top of Emmetts, but just short of the yard go right over the stile and follow the left-hand boundary and then cross a stile in the far left-hand corner of the field. In the next field follow the right-hand hedge and cross the stile on your right. (370m)

From the stile views of the amphitheatre of the Upper Wyre can be seen—the Ward's Stone ridge to your left and the Hawthornthwaite ridge to the right.

Over the stile cross the middle of the field towards a barn whose roof is visible from the stile. On your way you pick up a left-hand fence and cross a stile. Go past

47

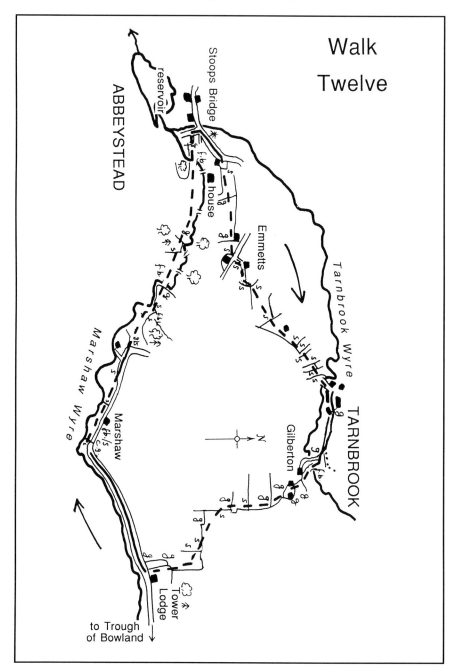

Walk Twelve

the right-hand side of the barn and the follow the right-hand fence to cross a stone stile in the far right-hand corner. In the next field follow the right-hand wall and fence to cross a stone gap or an A-stile in the corner and then cross the next stile to your left in the opposite side of the access lane. (1000m)

Cross the middle of the next field to a stile over the short wall in the fence and then, over this, go to cross the next stile in the wall facing you. Go through a stile by a gate at the bottom of the field after which cross the bridge over the Tarnbrook Wyre and then follow the enclosed track into the hamlet of Tarnbrook. (300m)

The houses of the hamlet are of interest for their vernacular features. The settlement is a 'closed village' being within the estate ownership. At one time it comprised twenty-five houses and employed a hundred hatters.

At the far end of the hamlet, go through the gate by the barn where the metalled road ends. Go along this farm and moorland access track, bear right at the fork to pass over the two cattle grids and go towards Gilberton Farm and the Wyre. (600m)

The signs for the access area remind you that the moors encircling you are private and public access is only allowed on a small proportion of 'access areas' where Lancashire County Council pays a tribute to owners and tenants and provides a ranger service.

Do not cross the Wyre by the farm access bridge but use the footbridge a few metres upstream. Continue ahead towards the wall at the rear of the farm and then go left along the track by this wall. Follow this track over a series of two arched bridges and two gates to arrive in a yard between two barns. (270m)

Bear right in the yard and leave by the right-hand gate. In the field go left and follow by the left-hand wall to pass through the gate in the fence across your way. Continue to climb up parallel to the wood to cross a stile in the top left-hand corner of the field. (300m)

Continue by the near the left-hand wall to pass through a prominent gate in the wall ahead. Continue towards the left-hand wall and cross it by the prominent iron ladder stile. (270m)

At the highest point of the walk you are on the edge of the moor. Any of these fields could, with neglect, revert to moor or, with care, become grassy fields again. Such is the balance of nature.

Over the stile go half right to cross the wooden ladder stile and then go half left to cross the similar stile over a fence and ruined wall. Over the stile go slightly right and downhill to pass the concrete bases of wartime army huts and aim to pass through the gate in the wall in the gap between the two woods. Follow the track down by the right-hand wall to Tower Lodge and, by a further stile and gate, the Trough of Bowland Road and the Marshaw Wyre. The Trough road can be seen climbing to its pass as you walk down towards the woods. (1000m)

Go right along the road and follow it until a cattle grid marks the end of the unenclosed section. (1470m)

The open section of road is a favourite picnic spot of motorists. The ageing Scots pine and oaks are benefitting from some new planting. Perhaps more could yet be done?

Do not cross the cattle grid but use the stile on the left to gain the riverside field. Follow the right-hand wall to a slab footbridge, cross the facing stile and then continue along the wall to a stile and small gate opposite a private bridge. Go over the stile and continue along the right-hand wall until, some 30 metres after it has given way to a fence, a further stile gives access to the road. (500m)

Go left on the road, ignore the left turn towards Scorton, and continue until the road bends sharp right. Rejoin the fields by the stile and gate and follow the left-hand boundary along until the wall bends left. Go towards the right-hand wood and then follow the fence down to the bottom where a small stream meets the Wyre. Cross the stile, footbridge and stile to another field. (620m)

Follow the left-hand fence, (ignoring the stile), and then the wall as it bends round, passes a field gate and leads to a kissing gate. Go through and cross the river by the footbridge. (250m)

Go forward in the field, letting the river meander to the right. After climbing past an old tree keep your height above the river, with the wood above you to the left. Continue above the river until, as the river swings towards you, opposite the private footbridge a series of stone steps to your left leads up to a stile and a short section of wood. Follow the right-hand fence, pass the stone bearing the date of planting (1908) in Lord Sefton's time of ownership and continue through the next kissing gate into the field. Keep near to but above the right-hand fence in this long field and gradually drop down towards the riverbank when opposite the house. (1000m)

Abbeystead House was built in 1886 by the then Earl of Sefton. It is Elizabethan in style, with mullioned and transomed windows and gables, and cost £100,000. One cynic dubbed it a 'palatial shooting box!'

Just after the grounds of the house is a substantial footbridge to cross the river. Use this and then the stile, turn left in the field and, after the wooden shelter, follow the left-hand fence of the field and then pass through the metal rail field gate before bearing right to reach the metalled road at Stoops Bridge. (370m)

When canal and railway held sway

Conder Green—Aldcliffe—Galgate—Conder Green

12 kilometres (7.5 miles) with a slightly longer route easily possible

Start: Conder Green Picnic Site (turn off the Cockerham Lancaster road by the Stork Hotel (GR 457561). O.S. Pathfinder map 659 (SD 45/55) Galgate and Dolphinholme and with a section on 648 (SD 36/46) Lancaster

THE WALK is mostly along the route of an old railway and a canal towpath with a quiet lane and fieldpaths between them. It is a walk for any season but the autumn colours in the canal cutting woods are glorious. The walk is the story of transport through the ages and has much wildlife particularly along the Lune Estuary. The walk is very suitable for those with little experience of pathfinding.

Instead of walking back through the fields from Galgate to Conder Green the walk can be extended along the canal, down the Glasson Branch to Glasson Dock, and then to Conder Green by the old railway track.

Conder Green station, the site of the car park, was opened on the Lancaster Glasson Dock branch railway in 1890, some seven years after the railway itself. The line carried passengers until 1930 and goods to the port until 1947. The lines were finally raised in 1962. The branches only claim to fame was in 1917 when King George V stayed overnight on the royal train shunted into Glasson.

Tales are told of firemen who used to kick out odd lumps of coal when passing a fishermen's hut and, in return, gained the occasional salmon. One driver was demoted after arriving at Lancaster only to find that he had left the carriages at Glasson.

From the picnic site car park, with the estuary on your left, go along the path that follows the trackbed of the railway until you meet the next information board and metalled road crossing your way beneath Aldcliffe. (4200m)

The building on your left after passing under the smoke-stained bridge is called Waterloo—no doubt a clue to when it was built. The railway line, before passing Ashton Hall golf course has the overgrown remains of the wooden platform built especially for Mr Starkie, the owner of the hall. A birdwatcher would do well to carry binoculars along this stretch.

Go right on the metalled road and climb through the attractive village of Aldcliffe. Go left at the road junction at the top of the village and follow the road down to meet the canal. Turn right and follow the towpath (with the water on your left) all the way until the first bungalows (on the left) of Galgate are reached between bridges 88 and 89 (unless you want the extension to the route mentioned in the introductory comments). (5400m)

This well-wooded section is attractive in spring and autumn. The canal passes through a three-kilometre cutting to avoid the need for locks. In fact the main canal from Preston to Tewitfield is devoid of locks—a distance of forty-eight kilometres. The bridges you pass under are fine examples of the work of the builder Rennie and one bridge you pass over syphons a stream under the canal.

Once opposite the first bungalows in Galgate look for a stone stile in the hedge on your right. Cross this and then go half right in the field to join the woodside now on your left. Cross the stile by the gate in the fence across your way and continue along the woodside to find an iron stile where the wood kinks inwards. (250m)

Cross this stile, follow the path up through the wood and leave by another iron stile. In the field climb straight ahead over the hillock with a pylon ahead. Descend the hillock to the left

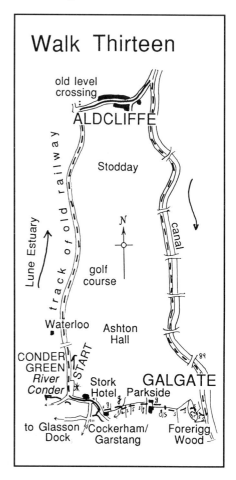

of the pylon and two hedgerow trees, in the facing boundary, to cross a further iron stile. (250m)

Follow the right-hand field boundary down, pass under the overhead transmission cables, and go over the stile adjacent to the gate on your right in the hedge. In the next field turn left and go down to the yard of Parkside Farm. Pass straight through the yard to find a stile by a gate in the boundary facing you at the far side of the yard. (370m)

Cross the stile and follow the right-hand boundary and continue likewise over the next stile. In the bottom right-hand corner, with Crow Wood on your right, cross the stile and then the stiled slab footbridge and then through the small gate on your right—all within a few metres of each other. In the field turn left and follow the left-hand boundary up through a gate and then down the next field to pass the rear of Webster's Farm to a stile by the small telephone exchange. (750m)

Use the stile to gain the road, turn right and go along to the Stork Inn and regain the car park down the side road along the River Conder. (800m)

From Beacon Fell

Beacon Fell—Blindhurst—Bleasdale—Beacon Fell

9 kilometres (5.5 miles)

Start: Beacon Fell—the eastern side Quarry car park is advised especially for those who might wish to omit a climb of the fell (GR 573428). O.S. Pathfinder map 668 (SD 44/54) Garstang

A N UNUSUAL WALK in that the start and finish given are the highest point of the walk. It affords good views of Bleasdale, the surrounding Bowland Fells, Longridge Fell and Pendle as well as south towards Darwen Moors and Winter Hill.

From the summit of Beacon Fell, using the indicator on the triangulation pillar, go eastward along the surfaced path and follow it all the way to the quarry car park. Continue down the access road and meet the road that circles the fell. Go left and then take the road that branches immediately right. (800m)

At the end of the wall on the left of this lane, some 20 metres from the junction, is a stile which you cross. In the field go half right, and towards the right-hand side of Parlick, and down to where a fence corner meets a rough track. Go left down the track. (250m)

Go along through a series of two gates with stiles, past a stile and gate on your left, and when the track bends right at the bottom of a field go ahead to climb the stile facing you. Follow the left-hand boundary down the next field towards, but not to cross, a further stile. (600m)

On the nearside of the stile turn right and follow the left-hand fence towards the rear of Wood Acre Farm. In the corner go over the stile by the gate on your left, turn right to pass the farm and then go to the farm access track through another gate on your right. (300m)

Go left down the track and right when it meets the road bend. Pass Watery Gate Farm and go through the gate on the left just before the roadside wood. In the field go to follow the left-hand fence along to a stile in the fence across your way in the far left-hand corner of the field. (380m)

Over the stile go half right to cross the field, aiming for the roof of Lower Core Farm, and go through the gate nearly opposite the barn to reach the road opposite the farm outbuildings. Go right up the road. (450m)

Go past the bungalow to reach and turn into the gated entrance track to Higher Core Farm on your left. Re-enter the fields by the first gate on your left along this track and follow the right-hand wall to the field corner. The corner is fenced—use the gate in this to pass through to the next field which is crossed by aiming for Blindhurst Farm ahead. (900m)

This leads you to a footbridge in the depression in the far right corner of the field. Over turn right and follow the stream and boundary until you see a short section of stone wall. Climb the stile in the wall and climb up to the farm which you reach after crossing the field and following the access track. (500m)

Blindhurst Farm has a 1731 datestone and its architectural style, with cross windows and three-lighted mullioned and transomed windows, reflects its age. There are two farmhouses opposite each other—it is said that two brothers fought over the same land, and when one brother built a house the other responded likewise.

Go left in the cobbled yard in front of the whitewashed farm, pass the stone house on your left and then go through the gates to your right between the stone outbuild-

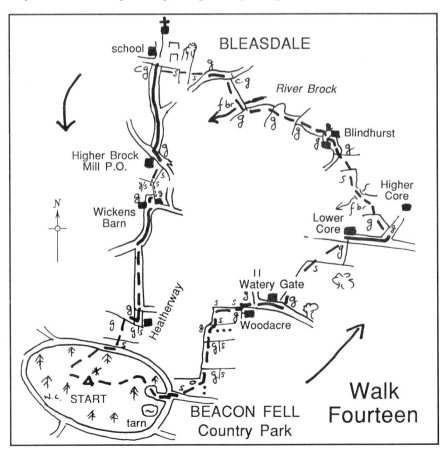

ings. Almost immediately after, and next to the blue slurry store, go through the next gate and follow the rough track down the field. Go through the left-hand of two adjacent gates in the bottom left-hand corner of the field. (260m)

The amphitheatre of Bleasdale and surrounding fells are seen to great advantage from Blindhurst.

In the next field follow the track near the right-hand fence, and when the fence bends away to the right cut across the field corner to pass through the nearby gate. Go towards the right-hand fence to pick up the infant River Brock and then pass through a gate in the section of stone wall and pass over the footbridge. (500m)

Follow the right-hand boundary and stream along to a road, go left and after a 100 metres the road bends left. Leave the road to pass through a gate in the right-hand corner. Cross the field aiming for the middle of the long conifer plantation ahead. (570m)

Cross the right-hand of two stiles, go straight through the narrow plantation, cross the next stile and follow the right-hand fence alongside the school playing field along to the road by the school. (240m)

The church and circle of Bleasdale lie to the right from here and details are given in Walk 4.

Turn left and go down the estate road to meet the public road at the bottom. Turn left to reach Brock Mill Post Office. (750m)

The post office is also a café—a favourite watering hole of cyclists and ramblers for many generations.

To return to Beacon Fell continue past the post office and climb up the road until a flight of steps enables you to cross a stile and re-enter the fields to the right. Follow the left-hand boundary to a gate and stile across your way. Cross here, turn left to cross the next stile, turn right and follow the fence along to pass through the yard of Wickens Barn Farm and reach the road. (520m)

Turn right along the road and just after the right-hand bend go left down the access road signed to Broadhead. When the track forks go straight ahead through the gateway and then cross a stile by a gate on your right opposite the house, where the drive bends left. (870m)

Follow the left-hand fence until a gate admits you to the field below Beacon Fell. Go left and climb straight up the field to cross a stile and, shortly above, the road that circles the fell. The quarry car park lies to the left. (380m)

If you go right on the road for 10 metres you will find a path on the left which climbs diagonally through the wood, crosses a track and then open fell to reach a broken wall. The wall climbs left to the summit. (390m to summit)

On the edge of the Bay

A: Pilling (Fluke Hall)—Preesall—Knott End—Fluke Hall

12 kilometres (7.5 miles)

B: Pilling (Fluke Hall)—Tongues—Pilling Lane—Fluke Hall

7.5 kilometres (4.5 miles)

Start: Fluke Hall, Pilling (GR 389500). Alternate starts from Preesall or Knott End are possible for the longer route. O.S. Pathfinder map 658 (SD 34/35) Fleetwood

A WALK ACROSS FIELDS, along the bed of the 'Pilling Pig' railway and along the coast using part of the Lancashire Coastal Way. A variety of scenery and a chance to see the local gastronomic speciality 'Pilling duck' being reared. The walk often gives the chance for seeing a variety of birds and super views across Morecambe Bay.

Routes A and B—Fluke Hall to Preesall.

LEAVE THE CAR PARKING AREA and go through the gate across the road opposite from the Lancaster Port Health Authorities notice. With your back to the gate, cross the middle of the field to a gate and, through, continue in the same directions between two gate posts and to the ruined site of a farm (Old Ridge) by following near the right-hand field boundary. Go through the gate to the left of the first ruin and then keep to the right of the ponds as you go half right to reach a gate in the facing boundary. (390m)

Go through the gate and, with your back to it, cross the field roughly parallel to the right-hand boundary, to arrive at the right of a couple of small trees in a rough patch of ground. Continue past these and, keeping in the same direction, continue down the field to a short footbridge over a fenced dyke. (370m)

Cross the bridge and turn right to follow the dyke to the far corner of the field. Here simply turn left and follow the right-hand boundary up to a gate in the top right-hand corner of the field. (450m)

Go through the gate and turn left down the track, alongside the left-hand hedge until a stile appears on your left, short of the left-hand corner. Do not cross but turn right here and pick up the left-hand field boundary of the same field, which you follow to a stile in the field corner. (700m)

Over the stile continue along the left-hand boundary to the footbridge facing you. Over go through the gate on the right and through follow the farm track to the left to reach a metalled road. (100m)

Go left on the road past Barnet Lee and reach Bibby's Farm on your right. (550m)

Enter the yard and pass directly between the farm outbuildings to a gate, through which you go to follow the left-hand fence around to a further gate. Through this go half right to cross the concrete road and cross the bridged dyke to the left of the gate to re-enter a field. In the field follow the long left-hand fence and dyke all the way down, through the gate facing you in the left-hand corner and then continue by a left-hand fence to cross the stile facing you in the field corner. (400m)

Pass through the rough patch and follow the left-hand fence around to a stile and track by Bourbles. Go right on the track that passes the house front to reach and pass through a gate. Here the shorter route leaves (see route B below). (250m)

For route A continue along the track but then go left after the first of two fishing pits (ignore the small fence). At the end turn right alongside the second pit and, towards the end, bear left to a stile in the fence. (100m)

Over the stile follow the right-hand boundary to a footbridge, cross this and then the next field to a small gate on the nearside of the nearest building—crossing the indiscernible line of the old railway in so doing. (250m)

Follow the left-hand fence through the garden, pass through the kissing gate and continue along the dyke to reach a track. Go right on the track, in front of the houses, and go down to meet the metalled road near the old level crossing gates. (450m)

Go left along the road but cross to a stile behind the bus shelter. Over this follow the left-hand fence to the next stile, cross and turn left and cross a further stile. Then go right to a footbridge over which you climb the hill near the left-hand fence to a further stile at the rear of the school. (500m)

Looking from the school you can look back over the way you have come and beyond the hills of the Forest of Bowland, or to the north and the fells of Lakeland.

Follow the enclosed path around the right-hand side of the school field to emerge on the road. Go right down School Lane to emerge on the main road by the Saracen's Head and Blackbull public houses. (230m)

Preesall to Knott End

WITH THE PUBS on your left go down the road until a bridge (Ford Stones) leads over the track bed of the old Garstang–Knott End railway line. Just over the bridge a small gateway on the left gives you access down to the track bed which you follow directly ahead for around a mile—ignoring any tracks or paths off to either side—until your way is blocked by a bungalow garden. (2000m)

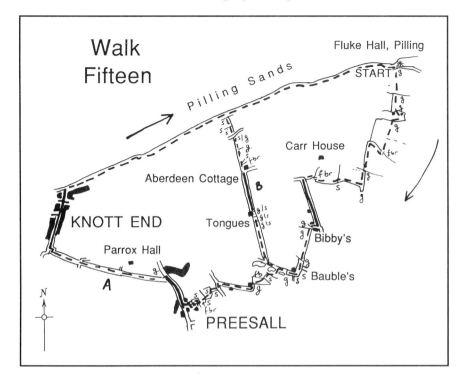

Walk
Fifteen

Fluke Hall, Pilling

Pilling Sands

START

Carr House

Aberdeen Cottage

KNOTT END

Tongues

Bibby's

Parrox Hall

Bauble's

N

A

PREESALL

To the right, from the railway, can be seen Parrox Hall, the Elizabethan house which has been the home of the Elletson family since the seventeenth century.

Go round the right of the bungalow on path and then turn right down Hackensall Road, cross the main road and go along Clarence Avenue to the sea wall and sands. (740m)

Knott End to Fluke Hall—along the Lancashire Coastal Path

WITH THE SANDS of Morecambe Bay on your left go along the sea wall embankment path to the small car park at Fluke Hall where you began. (4100m)

Route B

THROUGH THE GATE follow the track ahead but take the first branch right along Tongues Lane. Follow this lane along, through the three gates with stiles opposite the house and continue along the metalled section until it bends sharp right at Aberdeen Cottage. (1250m)

Your ways lies alongside the left-hand dyke and between all the buildings. Cross a footbridge after the narrow section of path and then continue by the dyke side, often with nettles, to reach and cross a stile. Over the stile continue along the left-hand fence to pass by a gate and continue ahead to join the road by a stile and gate. (420m)

Cross the road to a stone stile and follow the right-hand dyke-side path over three further stiles to reach the embankment. Turn right on the embankment to reach the start of the walk. (2270m)

Where the Wyre meets the sea

Knott End—Hackensall Hall—Barnaby's Sands—Curwen's Hill

6.5 kilometres (4 miles)

Start: The Ferry Pier (car park) at Knott End (GR 346484). O.S. Pathfinder map
658 (SD 34/35) Fleetwood

START FROM THE FERRY PIER at Knott End where, behind the café that was once the
terminus station for the Garstang to Knott End railway, there is a car park. The
walk follows, for its first stretch, the Wyre Way. This route encircles the estuary
between Knott End and Fleetwood.

With the estuary on your right begin to walk the signed path and arrive at Sea
Dyke, a cottage built in 1754. Turn in from the river here and immediately after the
house turn right off the more distinct track and follow the right-hand edge of the golf
course. Continue up the rise until your are above the sailing centre roof. (680m)

The view over the estuary to Fleetwood gives quite a dramatic skyline especially
on summer evenings when the high tide is up.

Leave the fence here and cross the links to aim for the near side of the timber
buildings in front of the trees that surround Hackensall Hall. (320m)

On the nearside of the wooden shed pick up a track and go along to the farm
buildings. Turn left at the junction, passing between the wood and outbuildings, and
then left by the house. (150m)

The hall dates back to 1656 but the Jacobean house was 'restored' in 1873. The
hall has various legends associated with it including one of skeletons being bricked
up in cavities. The name Hackensall is allegedly derived from the place where
Haakon, a Viking, landed from the Isle of Man to claim a home in the tenth century.

Take the track that goes right after the garden and follow this rough surface along,
across the golf course, ignore the road to the sewage works, past a windswept
woodland and arrive at a track bend just under two parallel overhead wire posts near
the edge of the estuary. Here we leave the Wyre Way. (1200m)

The ungrazed saltings are called Barnaby's Sands and, with the adjacent Burrows
Marsh, form a designated Site of Special Scientific Interest. The marshes are not only
criss-crossed with creeks but contain a delightful selection of plants typical of such a
habitat. The site is owned by ICI whose factory dominates the western shore of the
estuary.

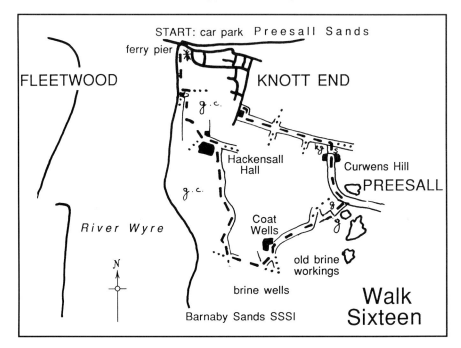

START: car park Preesall Sands

ferry pier

FLEETWOOD

KNOTT END

Hackensall
Hall

Curwens Hill

PREESALL

River Wyre

Coat
Wells

old brine
workings

N

brine wells

Barnaby Sands SSSI

**Walk
Sixteen**

Go left along the track and when the left-hand ruined hedge gets closest to the track leave it to go left across the small part of the field. Pass through the old gateway with its remnant gate post, go under the overhead wires and follow the right-hand hedge until it bends right. From here go towards Coat Wall Farm buildings using the track to the left to reach the farmyard. (370m)

In the yard go immediately right down the farm access track until it bends sharp left. Continue straight ahead across the next field to pick up a bend in the field boundary. Follow this (the hedge on your left) until you reach a gateway. Go through this and in the next field go right to follow the fence to reach a gate in the corner of the field. (780m)

This area is the site of the Preesall salt mines. All around are water-filled hollows of former mines and, nearer the Wyre, the well heads of the current brine extraction wells. The salt field was found in 1872 whilst prospecting for iron ore was underway. The ponds are subsidence of old wells and the mine and are now used by local fishermen.

Eventually the salt industry began and now forms part of the giant ICI company. The salt is electrolysed to make new chemical products including chlorine, hydrogen and sodium hydroxide. These in turn are used as chemicals or the basis for making other products such as PVC.

The area of the saltfield is roughly from the Wyre to Preesall and from near Knott End and towards Stalmine. Controlled solution and brine pumping, eventually under the Wyre, is the current method of extraction.

Through the gate go left up the track to reach the yard of Curwen's Hill Farm and its 1735 datestone. Pass by the right-hand side of the house, with a white-walled outbuilding on your right to reach a stile. Cross and go down the field to a small kissing gate and reach the track bed of the old railway. Go left, ignoring side tracks, and continue along the final wooded track bed until a fence blocks your way. (1490m)

Go right to pass around the bungalow and then right along Hackensall Road until a short path, by a seat, on your left leads you through to the next road. Go right, left into Parkway, right down Holmfield Road and left into Quail Holme Road, which you follow back to your starting point. (820m)

The Three Parishes Walk

St Michaels-on-Wyre—Great Eccleston—Inskip—St Michaels

14 kilometres (8.5 miles) with a shorter alternative of 10 kilometres (6 miles)

Start: St Michaels-on-Wyre Church (there is a car park by the school in Hall Lane) (GR 462409). Alternatively starts can be made from Inskip or Great Eccleston. O.S. Pathfinder maps 68 (SD 44/54) Garstang and 679 (SD 43/53) Preston (North)

T HIS WALK uses some quiet and unfrequented paths in the parishes of Inskip, Great Eccleston and Upper Rawcliffe with Tarnacre (St Michaels). It can be started from either of the three villages and the walk could be done in parts with the use of public transport. St Michaels Church is worth a visit. In winter many species of birds have been seen and views across to the Bowland Fells and Black Combe can be extensive.

The shorter route is from St Michaels to Great Eccleston and back, missing out Inskip.

Stage One: St Michaels to Great Eccleston.

FROM THE CHURCH cross the River Wyre by the footbridge and immediately, on the far bank, turn left to cross the main road with care and enter the riverside field by the kissing gate. (100m)

Follow the riverbank embankment top path along, through two further kissing gates and over two stiles, to reach the next road. Go right on the road and take the second of two left turns to Turnover Hall Farm. (1500m)

Go down the track, pass the bungalow and continue through the yard until a barn crosses your way. Turn right here, sometimes gated, and then first left, again gated, to follow the track towards open fields. The track bends sharp right with three adjacent gates on your left. Your way lies to enter the fields by third gate. (100m)

In the field follow the long left-hand fence and continue along when a track joins from the left. Go through the two consecutive gates, pass the left-hand pond and cross the stile by the gate in the far left-hand corner of the next field at the end of the track. Continue by the left-hand boundary past the larger pond to cross the next stile just beyond the pond. (370m)

Again continue along the left-hand boundary, towards the farm with the silo tower, until a gate enables you to cross through into the field on your left. In this field go right to cross the gated farm bridge and head towards the silo tower at Wildboar Farm. Go through the left-hand of two gates, cross the farm access track and re-enter the field by gate at the left-hand side of the silo tower. (450m)

From here go through the gate ahead and towards the right-hand corner of the field. Cross this next field by aiming for the gap between the right of the bungalow and barn, cross two consecutive stiles and then following the road ahead, passing Fir Tree Farm (kennels) and on to Crabtree Farm. (750m)

Just short of this last farm the track bends left. Go round this bend but leave the track immediately through a gate on your right by an oak tree. In the field follow the right-hand boundary, passing the farmhouse, and over the stile in the right-hand corner. Continue along the right-hand boundary in the next field to a further stile which you cross. (480m)

Go left on this track, pass through the farm buildings and then go left on the road. Soon an aqueduct and adjoining footbridge enable you to cross the Wyre again. On the far bank follow the crest of the embankment to your left. (530m)

After two stiles a gate appears in the fence on the left. Opposite this gate drop down right into the field and cross the stile by the gate on the right of the squat, square building. A short lane then takes you to the A586. Great Eccleston centre lies across and to the right—where refreshments can be found. (1000m to A586)

Stage Two: Great Eccleston to Inskip.

FROM THE POINT at which you met the A586 go left, eastward, and follow the road along but crossing to the far side when safe to do so. Turn right down the first road off, White House Lane, and then first left down Moss Side Lane. Follow this twisting lane until it ends at Fiddlers Farm. (1500m)

Go over the stile between the barn and gate and then go down the field to cross a stile, a short enclosed path with newly planted trees and then cross over the footbridge in the far right-hand corner. Continue by the right-hand boundary, with a huge vehicle repair yard to your right, and then go through the gate in the corner. (450m)

Turn left along the track, pass Hollyovenbeck and continue through the gate ahead along the track through two gates to re-enter a field. Here follow the right-hand boundary along to pass the huge factory farm buildings to the footbridge. (See stage four for the shorter route to St Michaels). (490m)

To continue to Inskip turn right to cross the footbridge and follow the ditch that runs alongside the buildings and along to the farmhouse. (130m)

Go through the gate facing you and then pass through a further gate almost directly ahead. In the next field cut across to the left-hand boundary by the pond. Follow this

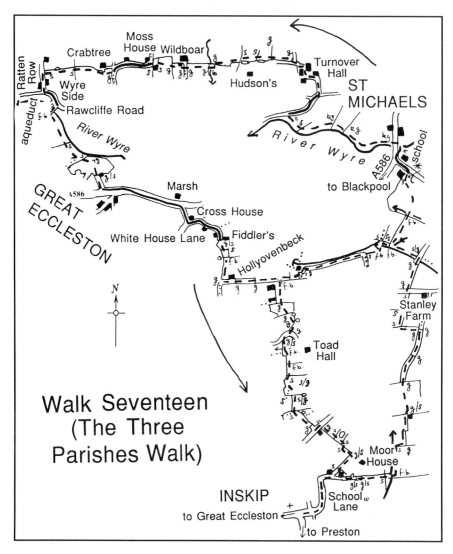

Walk Seventeen
(The Three
Parishes Walk)

boundary along to cross a stile by an old gateway. Follow the right-hand boundary to a gate and a road. Cross the road diagonally right to cross the stile by the gate and footpath sign (with the old railway wagon behind). (310m)

In the field follow the right-hand hedge, cross the footbridge, continue straight ahead near the right-hand boundary, over a smaller footbridge and then continue by the right-hand boundary towards a stile in the far right-hand corner of the field. Do not cross this stile but turn left to follow the fence around the pond to cross a stile by a gate on your right. (700m)

In the next field go directly ahead to a stile with white tops by the pond on your left. Cross the next stile and continue along the right-hand hedge in the next field, cross the double stile in the corner, and then follow the left-hand hedge to a stile and gate to reach a road. (620m)

Turn left on the road but pass through the first gate on the right, just after the house. In the field follow the right-hand ditch along to a stile, continue near the ditch with a pond on your left and cross the stile at the end of this small, rough enclosure. (110m)

In the next field follow the right-hand boundary but in less than 10 metres go right over a stile and small stone footbridge. In the field go left to cross the stile by the gate in the corner. Over the stile turn immediately right and cross the other stile and then follow the right-hand boundary along to a stile and a short enclosed path between houses. (450m)

At the end of the path is School Lane. Go right to Inskip or left to return to St Michaels.

Stage Three: Inskip to St Michaels

FROM INSKIP CHURCH go along into School Lane. At the end of School Lane lies Skitholme Cottage where the lane bends sharp left to a farm. Continue directly ahead and after two stiles by gates re-enter the fields. (250m from where the path in the paragraph above joins School Lane)

Go along the left-hand hedge, cross the stile, pass through the small wood and pass over the footbridge at the far side. Turn left to follow the dyke side, pass over the stile in the field corner and then turn right to follow the hedge to the next field corner. Ignore the gate to the right and turn left to follow the edge of the wood along. Continue along the right-hand hedge and cross over the combined stile and gate in the far right-hand corner by the small building. (900m)

In the next field cross the middle so that you are walking in the same direction as in the previous field and aiming for the right-hand corner of a long wood. Pass through the gate in this corner and then follow the concrete farm road along. (870m)

Leave the road by the fourth gate on your left, just short of a further gate that crosses the track. In the field follow the right-hand hedge and then turn right over the stile when the hedge gives way to a fence. Continue along the old right-hand hedge line to cross two further stiles before you reach the road. (320m)

Cross the road almost directly to a gate and then follow the right-hand boundary down the field to a gate and cross the brick bridge. Immediately on the far side go left through the stile by the gate and follow the dyke along to the wood at the far side.

Continue through the wood, and just before the dykes join go right over the footbridge. (750m)

Go straight down the field by following the left-hand hedge, where the short cut of section four joins this route, along to cross a footbridge in the far left-hand corner. (380m)

In this last field before St Michaels aim for the school and pick up the short enclosed path by the school side to reach the road. Go left and then right at the junction to the church. (380m)

Great Eccleston to St Michaels—Shorter Route.

FROM THE CORNER of the buildings ignore the footbridge to the right and continue along the right-hand hedge through into the second field. Just after the overhead lines cross the field, cut across the corner of the field to a small footbridge and stile (about 30 metres from the right-hand corner). Cross these, follow the left-hand boundary for about a further 30 metres to cross the stile, on your left where the hedge gives way to a fence. Go directly across the small paddock, pass through the gate and then follow Thatcher House's access track to the right and along parallel to the left-hand trees and ditch. Continue along the track until it bends sharp right. (1000m)

Leave it here to cross the stile facing you and continue along near the ditch and then cross the footbridge over the watercourse. On the far bank go over the right-hand of two stiles and follow the rough ditchside along to cross a further stile behind the pipe. Over this turn left through the small corner woodland and go along the left-hand hedge of the field where you join the route from Inskip in stage 3. (270m)

St Michael's Church is described by Pevsner as a typical medieval north-country church. The tower dates from around 1549. In 1956 an early fourteenth-century painting of the Ascension was discovered on the north wall. The church, with its low and dark interior, was rebuilt in 1611 and also has some fourteenth-century glass fragments.

Exploring Barnacre

Garstang—Barnacre—Garstang
7 kilometres (4.5 miles)
Start: The Community Centre Car Park, Garstang (GR 493454). O.S. Pathfinder
map 668 (SD 44/54) Garstang

THIS WALK uses several of the paths used in previous walks but links together Lady
Hamilton's Well, Barnacre Church, Greenhalgh Castle and a section of the canal.
A few short cuts can be made back to Garstang.

With the River Wyre on your right, walk around the edge of the playing field to
the water intake and bridge over the river. Here North West Water extracts water
from the Wyre, augmented from the Lune, and just beyond is the flood prevention
dam. (370m)

Climb the steps on the stone wall and cross the river. Just after the small road
junction go down the banking on the left to enter the field by a stile and cross to the
next stile. Over this continue in the same direction, with Nicky Nook Fell ahead, to
find and cross a further stile. (370m)

In this next field cut across to the far hedge and follow this, on your left, to a stile
and gate. Over here go right on the lane, keep left at the fork and go up to join the
metalled road. (620m)

Go left along the road but at the end of the first field after the farm on the right
is a stiled footbridge. Use this to enter the field and follow the left-hand hedge along
to a further stile which puts you on a railway crossing—please take care. Over the
stile at the far side go to climb the footbridge over the motorway and on the far side
go up the field to pick up and follow a left-hand hedge to a stile and gate to gain
access to the lane beyond. (760m)

Go right on the lane, pass the cottage but when opposite the farm on the right go
through a gate and down a small enclosed track to the left. At the bottom, just over
the streamlet, cross the stile to the right and go half left towards the near side of the
wood ahead—in so doing you pass above Lady Hamilton's Well partially hidden by
hollies. (see walk 2) (300m)

In the left-hand fence by the side of the wood is a stile which you cross and then
follow the woodside steeply up the field. After the short rise go diagonally right, pass
the former Delph quarry below to your right, and find a stile at the far end of the

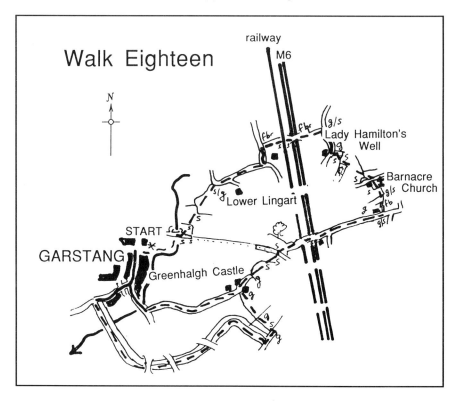

fence that continues on from the wall to your left. Whilst you pause for a breath on top of the rise look across to the Lakeland peaks. (250m)

Over the stile go down and along to the footbridge. Cross this and climb the steps to emerge at Barnacre Church with its stained glass windows of saints. If the church is open it is worth taking a few minutes to look inside. From the steps cross the road to a short flight of steps and then follow the short enclosed path to emerge, by a stile, into fields behind the church. (130m)

Follow the left-hand fence by the small wood to a further stile and gate. Once over continue along the left-hand boundary, pass two gates and then go through a further gate beyond to cross the stile and short concrete footbridge on your left. In the field go right to a stile and gate, over which turn right down Parkhead Lane. The lane goes down, keeping right at the fork, to cross the motorway, along with a small stream, and then the railway. (900m)

Go into the field to the left of the wood by the concrete stile. In the field go half right, pass along near the left-hand fence, and cross to a stile where the hedge gives way to a fence. Over this is a seat in a cutting of the former Garstang and Knott End railway. The area to the left, with stile access, is a memorial nature reserve. Drop down carefully and then climb the far bank to cross another stile. (260m)

A brief route can be made by following the line of the railway track to Garstang.

Cross the facing field to cross a further stile. In the field go right and follow the fence to a gate and then up to the yard of Greenhalgh Castle Farm. (380m)

Just beyond the seventeenth-century stone farmhouse the track leads to a stile on the right which enables you to visit the castle ruins. This is on private land so check with the farm first. The castle was built in 1490 by the first Earl of Derby and it was one of the last two strongholds in Lancashire to hold out against parliament in the Civil War.

Returning to the farm access drive you can either follow it right into Garstang or better still, but slightly longer, cross the track to the left-hand of three gates (the one nearest the farm) and go through to follow the right-hand hedge side to the next gateway. Go through and continue in almost the same direction to reach a plank and stile in the hedge facing you. Over go right, through the gate and go to the bridge over the canal down a short enclosed track. (750m)

Go over the bridge and down right to join the canal towpath. With the canal on your right you can go along to the Garstang Tithebarn basin crossing Rennie's famous Wyre aqueduct on your way. (2000m)

Nether Wyresdale Fell and Dale

Scorton—Dolphinholme—Harrisend Fell—Scorton

16 Kilometres (10 Miles)

Start: Scorton Village Centre.

O.S. Pathfinder maps: 668 (SD 44/54) Garstang and
659 (SD 45/55) Galgate and Dolphinholme

THIS ROUTE explores both the Wyre valley and open fellside before dropping back to Scorton. It is a walk of contrasts and deserves a good day to appreciate the varied views. The contrast between the river of the dipper and the open fell of the curlew add to the delights of the walk.

Leave Scorton village centre and walk down the road towards the Trough of Bowland and leave the houses behind. When the road bends slightly right to climb and cross the motorway, follow a signed path to the left. Go down the obvious path and then right over the footbridge and follow the enclosed route along until it leads to a stile on your right just over a double arched bridge. (800m)

Cross the stile and turn left to cross the footbridge in the field, and then aim for the rusty shed and cross over the stile by the gate. Go to the left of the shed and follow the left-hand edge of the field, by the watercourse, around to cross a further stile in the farthest left-hand corner of the field. (370m)

Follow the enclosed path, climb the steps at the end and then go right along the track to reach the road by the bridge over the River Wyre. (620m)

From this bridge follow the route of walk 10 upstream until you reach the bridge in Dolphinholme. (430m)

Continue over the bridge and climb the road up past Wagon Road Wood until the first track goes off to the left, to Dolphinholme House Farm. Go down this track, ignoring the left branch to the farmstead, and continue over a cattle grid and along through a gate at the fork in the track. Follow the twin tarred track across the field, go over the cattle grid and continue on the track by the right-hand hedge until the track bends right. (1300m)

Leave the main track here and go straight ahead through the facing gate and continue along the right-hand fence and go to cross over the gate in the far right-hand corner of the field. (320m)

In this next field contour around above the river valley and then bear right to pass through a gate in the field boundary across your way. Go ahead to pass the left-hand side of the barn and then continue directly ahead with a line of old hedgerow trees to your right. (500m)

Go through the gate facing you and climb up the field towards the farm buildings of Lower Swainshead. Enter the yard by the gate, continue directly ahead through the further gates between the buildings, and then turn right after the stone barn to follow the farm access track uphill. The track leads up to Swainshead Farm. Go left around the main buildings to continue along the tarred access track, called Waste Lane, to reach the road. (1800m)

Cross the road directly, pass through the gate and continue along the left-hand boundary of the field to pass through a gate in the far left-hand corner. Continue along the line of the old track down to cross a stream and then up to a ruined farm and a gate beyond. Through the gate go down to cross a further stream and, following the left-hand fence, continue up and along the track to a further ruined farm and a gate beyond. (810m)

Continue beyond the gate, but the track almost immediately bends right. Leave it here to go left through the old gateway and follow the left-hand boundary, and soon a small stream, uphill to reach the open moorland by a stile. From here the path is well waymarked by posts as first it climbs beside the left-hand fence. (520m)

When the fence bends left go forward to the marker post and then turn right to follow the narrow, waymarked path across the moorland until it eventually emerges on the road over Harrisend Fell. (1400m)

The moor is the home of grouse and curlew. There is even a patch of cranberry besides the path. The views down to Morecambe Bay make this an ideal walk for a clear day.

On reaching the unfenced road turn right and go downhill until a short marker post on the left, just before the road crosses a small stream, indicates where you turn. Cross the rough open ground with the stream to your right and eventually, almost at the far corner of the open land, you can cross a stile by a gate and re-enter a field. (700m)

Go towards the right-hand side of the farm ahead to find a gate in the fence across your way. In the next field follow the right-hand fence down to cross a stile in the lower right-hand field corner. In this last field before Sykes Farm, aim for the farm and cross a stile and the road directly opposite the farm access drive. (520m)

Go up towards the farm, turn left in the yard just after the house, and then right again. Go between these buildings to a gate and re-enter a field. Go directly across the middle of the field and then go to cross a stile in the far right-hand corner. In the next field go half left towards a single oak tree and then climb the hill in the field by following the line of old oaks upwards. (700m)

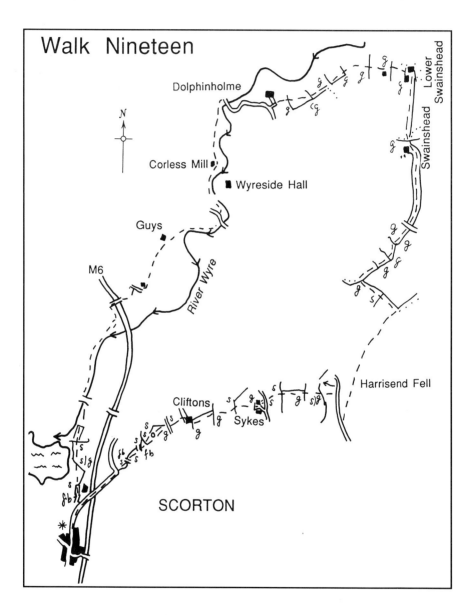

Walk Nineteen

Dolphinholme

Corless Mill

Wyreside Hall

Guys

M6

River Wyre

Lower Swainshead

Swainshead

Harrisend Fell

Cliftons

Sykes

SCORTON

From the last tree in the line go through the gate to your left and follow the right-hand fence down to a gate and the yard of Cliftons Farm. Go down through the yard below the house, turn right after the stone barn and go through the elaborate gate that leads to the farm access track. (370m)

Just beyond the gate go left over a stile by the field entrance and continue down this field to cross a stile at the mid-point of the next boundary across your way. Cross the access road and go through the rickety gate beyond. (190m)

In this field pass the ruins to the left and then climb the stile behind the small pond. Keep above the stream in the next field to find a further stile and, after crossing a short field, cross a further stile. Continue by the left-hand fence, cross the footbridge to your left, and continue between the wood and stream, over a stile and cross the next footbridge. (700m)

From here go across the remaining short piece of field and cross the stile to reach a road which, if followed left, soon leads over the motorway and down to Scorton. (1100m)

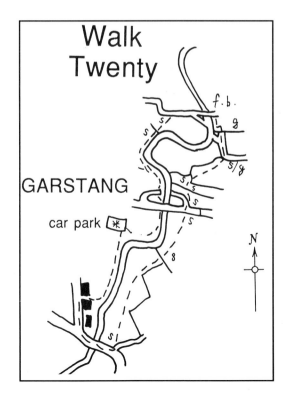

A short amble around Garstang

3.5 Kilometres (2 miles)

Start: The Community Centre car park at the north end of Garstang's High Street
(GR 493454) O.S. Pathfinder map 668 (SD 44/54) Garstang

THIS IS JUST A SHORT AMBLE on the edge of Garstang to while away a spare hour.
The walk is on paths well used by local people but might serve as a short amble
for visitors to the town. In wet weather a couple of the paths used can become rather
wet underfoot.

From the car park go forward to the riverbank and walk upstream by the riverside
path to the bridge and water intake over the River Wyre. Go under the bridge and
climb the embankment. Descend to the riverbank path which is followed, over a small
footbridge, to eventually reach a stile. From the stile follow the left-hand fence to a
further stile and over to reach a road. (1020m)

Go right on the road, but immediately after the double gate go left along the short
enclosed path and cross the river by the footbridge. On the far bank turn right and
follow the field edge down to a gate, and gain the track which is a continuation of
Wyre Lane which fords the river. (250m)

Go straight ahead, but when the track bends left go over the stile on the right of
the corner. Follow the right-hand boundary until it begins to bend right, and then
cross the field to an obvious stile. Over this aim for the right of the church tower with
a spire, to cross a further stile and, continuing in the direction of the spire go to cross
a further stile which gives access to the embankment. (700m)

Go right on top of the embankment but cross to go down over a stile on your
left. (30m)

In the field walk parallel to the river on your right to cross yet another stile across
your way. Continue near the left-hand fence, but when it bends left keep ahead on
the higher part of the field, and cross this large field by aiming to the left side of the
Wyre Bridge where you cross a further stile. (700m)

Over this stile go right over the bridge and pass the first few buildings before a
small track leads off right to the riverbank immediately after the bus garage. This
riverbank path goes directly back to the start of the walk. (600m)